ID0975166

Also by John M. Capozzi

Why Climb The Corporate Ladder
When You Can Take The Elevator?
500 Secrets for Success in Business and Life

If You Want The Rainbow . . . You Gotta Put Up With The Rain
500 Secrets for Success in Business and Life

John Capozzi donates 100% of the royalties from the sale of the
above books to educational scholarships for high risk and
disadvantaged children.

A Spirit of Greatness

THE BASIS

A Spirit of Greatness started with a phone call to an outstanding American Airlines reservationist—Mark Hawkins. I was struck by his proficiency, his attention to detail, and his genuine interest in ensuring that my trip would go well. My wife, LaDonna, and I are former AAers, so I never miss an opportunity to compliment a colleague. When I did, Hawkins replied, "Mr. Capozzi, I try to treat every customer as if they owned the company."

I wrote to Bob Crandall, then chairman of American, and told him that there had to be many others like Mark Hawkins, who daily go the extra mile for American and know of others who do so, too. In a 70-year-old company, in an exciting business like an airline, there had to be thousands of "great stories" out there. Bob agreed, and asked employees to share them with me.

The response was overwhelming: I received almost 4,000 letters from employees—from the maintenance shop floor to the corner offices. Only 12 were negative.

I wasn't surprised at this outpouring. American employees have a deeply ingrained pride in their company, their jobs, and their ability to make a difference in the lives of their customers and co-workers. What's more, they want everyone else to know what makes their airline great!

The letters speak of the dedication of AA's people to their customers and their tasks, of their integrity, their ingenuity, and their genuine interest in their customers and co-workers. In short, they speak to a desire to be, truly, "Something Special in the Air."

This kind of esprit de corps doesn't happen overnight. It develops over years—nurtured by leaders who inspire the best in people, provide the tools, and lead by example.

The American Airlines Story

The history of American Airlines is a rich one, full of extraordinary pioneers, innovators, strong chief executives and more "firsts" than seem possible. It traces back to Charles Lindbergh, who, in 1926, flew a bag of mail in a DH-4 biplane from Chicago to St. Louis on the first regularly scheduled flight of Robertson Aircraft Corporation, a forerunner of American Airways, which later became American Airlines. AAers frequently like to tell you that Charles Lindbergh was once "one of us."

From that first regularly scheduled mail service came more "firsts:"

■ American Airways introduced stewardesses to the skies in 1933, flying 18-passenger Curtiss Condor aircraft.

■ In 1934, Cyrus Rowlett Smith—"Mr. C.R."—was elected president of American Airlines, a post he would hold for 40 years. Smith was instrumental in the design of a revolutionary new airplane, the DC-3, which debuted in 1936.

■ American introduced the first air travel card in 1934—now considered the predecessor of today's credit card.

- American was the first airline to introduce scheduled domestic U.S. freight service (1944).

- By 1949, American had become the first airline in the United States to fly a full fleet of pressurized passenger airplanes.

- American was the first airline to launch nonstop transcontinental service between California and New York, with a DC-7 (1953), and the first to launch transcontinental jet service, using the new Boeing 707s (1959).

- American was also the first to embrace technology in the airline reservation business—starting with the Magnetronic Reservisor in 1952, to keep track of seats available on flights. This technology would later develop into SABRE, the largest civilian, real-time, electronic data processing system in the world. Today, more than 100,000 SABRE terminals track and book airline reservations in 70 countries around the world.

- American invented yield management, which allows airlines to predict more accurately customer loads, and efficiently allocate seats on every flight, giving customers more discount seats while maximizing airline revenues—a "win-win" for travelers and airlines.

- American was the first to introduce special fares—like the Family Fare Plan—as long ago as 1948, to encourage more people to fly. In 1977, American introduced Super Saver fares to stimulate discretionary travel.

■ In 1981, American introduced the AAdvantage program, the first airline customer loyalty program. It has been widely emulated by other airlines, but none has matched the success of AAdvantage, which today boasts 31 million members worldwide.

While American's accomplishments during its first 50 years were impressive, they pale in comparison to the company's rapid growth and continuing innovation since 1978, when Congress deregulated the U.S. airline industry.

American, burdened by an inefficient route system and high costs built up during the regulated era, found itself operating in a free-wheeling, brutally competitive, wide-open industry. Once again, it rose to the challenge, and, since 1978, has grown almost ten-fold—establishing itself along the way as a powerhouse in the world airline industry.

American capitalized on the hub-and-spoke system—opening hubs in Dallas/Fort Worth, Chicago, Miami and San Juan—and now operates one of the strongest domestic route systems in the industry.

The airline grew internationally, as well, taking over Eastern Airline's Latin American routes in 1990, and TWA's European routes in 1991. Innovative labor agreements allowed American to triple its fleet between 1978 and 1990; it now operates one of the youngest and most fuel-efficient fleets in the world. And employment has grown, from 38,000 in the mid-1970s to almost 100,000 employees today.

Through it all, the company has never lost sight of the

fundamentals of being a successful airline: attention to detail, the willingness to innovate, a passion to be the best, and great people. The company understands that its employees *are* American Airlines, so it seeks out the best, trains them intensively, demands the best from them and rewards them for their contributions to the company's success.

For example, American was the first airline to introduce profit-sharing—to allow employees to share in the company's good years—and in 1998, paid its employees a total profit-sharing fund of $250 million, the largest ever paid by any airline.

It is the only airline with a world-class suggestion program that rewards employees for safety-enhancing and cost-saving ideas: the company's IdeAAs in Action program has saved American over $470 million and has paid out more than $70 million to employees since its inception in February 1987. To date, the program has received more than 300,000 IdeAAs.

It rewards employees who provide great service—allowing customers to acknowledge the extra effort of individual employees.

It focuses on leadership, inviting employees to participate in any number of leadership programs; to sharpen their skills; to become better at what they do.

It demands attention to detail—as one of our letter-writers points out, "This is American Airlines ... if there's any doubt about this plane, it will stay here at JFK and American will put all the passengers on another plane ... and I mean it."

And management encourages participation and feedback, both positive and negative, from employees. From C.R. Smith to Albert Casey to Bob Crandall to Don Carty—American's senior executives are known for their accessibility; their willingness to listen; their desire to learn from the people who do the work. The most popular forums for these exchanges are the annual President's Conferences, held more than 25 times across the American system, and attended by thousands of employees who want to meet and talk with "the boss" each winter and spring.

The result: a strong sense of ownership and pride in the American Airlines name . . .

. . . which translates to people who truly do make the difference.

And here are their stories:

ABOVE AND BEYOND

All Our Passengers Are First Class

At the airport, when assigned to the "First Class check-in" position, it is customary for agents to assist the Economy check-in line when there are no First Class passengers.

On many occasions, passengers who are next in line hesitate to approach when called, explaining, "Ma'am, I'm not traveling First Class." My reply, "All American Airlines passengers are First Class; we just don't have that many seats in front," always brings a smile.

Lurain Murray
Passenger Service Agent
Montego Bay, Jamaica

Little Things *Do* Mean a Lot

I've always held the belief that the little deeds never go unnoticed and my experience with American Airlines surely proves this belief.

I was employed by American in Los Angeles from 1969 to 1984 as a facilities maintenance mechanic in Plant Maintenance. I consider these years to be some of the finest times of my life. I worked with wonderful people and I not only enjoyed my job, I relished it.

I had been with the company for about three years when I began to notice something that bothered me. It actually made me a bit sad. Over the months, people's baggage tags, lots of them, had been disconnected from their luggage and were just laying on the floor under and around the baggage belt line. It wasn't that we were being extra rough on the bags; normal handling had caused some of the identification tags to come off. Some of them were quite nice, leather and all, and they obviously cost some passenger a lot of money.

I was also concerned that the customer might think poorly of us, "If that's how they treat my luggage . . . " So, I decided to fix the problem "my way." I started to pick up the tags and take them home. I wrote a little note of apology to the passenger and I mailed the tag back. It was only a luggage tag and I never expected anyone would take the time to write me back, but soon some people did start to write. One letter was from a senior executive of General Motors who said he had a bad experience on American Airlines and had told his travel people never to book American again. Then he got his luggage tag back and he said my letter changed his mind about my company.

My letter paid off for the company. I felt great. I remember using the word "gotcha!" Getting a big guy from General Motors to rejoin my company was really something. I sent back all sorts of tags to lots of people. One that really floored me was a tag for Werner von Braun who became a head engineer for NASA.

As I started getting back letters, what I didn't know was that many more were being sent directly to American Airlines headquarters.

One day my supervisor came to me and told me I had to report to Mr. Ray Unangst's office. He ran Los Angeles Airport for American. I didn't know if I had done something wrong or what. When I got there, Mr. Robert Sullins, my foreman, was with Mr. Unangst and they presented me with a "Customer Comes First" award and a very elegant wristwatch. To this day, I cherish both very much.

So, I guess the moral of this story is, "Little things do mean a lot" and, "Anyone, no matter what your job, can really make a difference."

I am now retired and I live on a mountaintop in Oregon. I live right under a flight path for planes going to Seattle. When I see the obvious silver craft go by I always say, "There goes American." Every time, it makes me think back and remember those great days. I get such a warm feeling. From the bottom of my heart, I really miss those times and my friends. I'd like to say to the people working there now, you are more than the best, you are the finest.

Ron S. Holthouser
Retired Facilities Maintenance Mechanic
Los Angeles

"Can Do" Spirit

I was returning to Dallas/Fort Worth from Colorado Springs after a skiing weekend on a Fokker 100 flight that was completely full. Our flight attendant was working very hard to serve meals but unfortunately, as we started our descent to Dallas, she had not finished. The cabin needed to be picked up for landing.

The captain made an announcement that our approach to Dallas/Fort Worth would be delayed so that the Main Cabin meal service could be completed.

Suddenly an amazing thing happened. Eight employees who were traveling as non-revenue passengers stood up. They all had flight attendant training and assisted the flight attendant in completing the service.

The atmosphere was electric. Our customers were very impressed and we landed at DFW on time.

I think this is a wonderful example of the "can do" spirit of our employees. They certainly didn't have to help out, but they did. We could have simply arrived late, but all of us know how important it is to our customers to be on time. I was very proud to be a member of the AA family on that flight.

John E. Jaynes
Managing Director,
Food & Beverage Services/Duty Free
Headquarters

Amazing Courage

Not long ago, I received an incident report from the captain of a 727 that was scheduled out of Tulsa. The crew had just completed their pre-flight and were starting their engines checklist. The weather wasn't great, 35 degrees with blowing snow and severe wind gusts.

Suddenly, there was a loud crash directly in front of the plane. Not 20 feet in front of the cockpit, the crew observed the driver of a company pick-up truck crawling out of his now severely damaged truck. The remains of a 30-foot wood maintenance platform were littered all over the truck and surrounding area.

The platform had broken loose in the high wind and was about to crash directly onto the cockpit of the 727. The driver of the pick-up spotted the danger, and without a moment's hesitation, drove his truck directly into the platform to prevent its impacting the jet.

The driver asked to remain anonymous, but clearly, his unselfish actions prevented severe damage to one of our jets, and certainly prevented possible injury to our crew.

On behalf of all of us, we wish to thank our fellow employee for his amazing courage.

Captain Cecil D. Ewell, Jr
Chief Pilot
Vice President, Flight

I Take My Customers Seriously

Several months ago I received a somewhat frantic call from a marketing executive who urgently needed information on the American AAdvantage Miles program for an incentive program for one of her company's biggest clients. After discussing the preliminaries of the program, she hung up satisfied with the information we had discussed. However, over the next few days she called with more questions. We had trouble connecting and were forced to rely on voicemail. After what became a comical amount of "misses," and sensing the urgency of her last message, I left her my home phone number. When the customer called back the next day she expressed her amazement that I had given a customer my home phone number!

To me, good customer service is about taking your job and your customers seriously—this customer ultimately pays my salary, so giving her my home number is really no big deal. Understanding her needs and responding with commitment and enthusiasm *is* a big deal.

> Missy Fain
> National Account Manager
> AAdvantage Incentive Marketing
> Headquarters

Educational Outreach

Mr. Don Carty
President
American Airlines

Mr. Carty,

I have a strong need to share a recent experience with you regarding several people employed by American Airlines.

Back in October, I approached Linda Sivilich, who is a ticket agent at Philadelphia International Airport for American Airlines. My request was of a personal nature. I told Linda that I was in charge of the *Challenge* course in my children's grade school, Nativity B.V.M. in Media, PA. This program takes approximately twelve 7th and 8th grade students, who have obtained a consistent "A" average, and show learning maturity, in a small group environment. The goal of the *Challenge* program is to introduce the children to a variety of professions. Unlike the "usual" individual career days, this program asks people from various careers to join the children for an extended period of time (e.g. one hour on each Monday morning for eight weeks). I asked Linda if she could help me obtain a person, from American Airlines, who could spend eight 1-hour sessions with our children, explaining how the airline functions and operates. Linda did a lot of thinking, working and coordinating and contacted Bill Lokes, an American

Airlines pilot assigned to Kennedy Airport in New York, who is also involved with the mentor program. Linda continued to develop what was a most educational, informative and well-received program for our children. Linda, working with Bill Lokes, arranged for the following speakers to talk to our children:

- Week one—Bill Lokes brought in a flight plan and spoke to our children about the experience and educational background required to be a pilot. He also provided them with examples of tasks that pilots must do prior to and during flights.
- Week two—Linda Sivilich introduced the children to the variety of tasks and responsibilities required to get people ticketed and to their destinations.
- Week three—a general manager from another airline spoke to the children about what is required to operate an airline, from an upper management perspective.
- Week four—Fernando Viega, fleet service clerk, showed a video and impressed the children with the importance of maintaining and safely landing the airplanes.
- Week five—Chuck McGlynn, ramp supervisor, reinforced Fernando's message, indicating that everyone must do their jobs thoroughly and completely, in order to operate a safe and efficient airline.
- Week six—Nick Cicali, general manager, who has been with American Airlines for over 30 years, provided the children with an excellent perspective as to how the airline has evolved and changed, and fo-

cused on how the departments and people work together for a common goal.

- Week seven—Pat Marcella and Diane Kolodziejski, flight attendants, provided the children with a very interesting overview of the numerous tasks, situations and responsibilities associated with being flight attendants. They were very candid about the situations that they encountered. They stressed the importance of safety for crew members and their passengers.
- Week eight—Linda Sivilich arranged for the children to have a tour at the Philadelphia Airport, and what an excellent conclusion this trip was to the program. The volunteer tour guide did an excellent job of taking us through the airport and onto a plane. He also impressed the children with the importance of having a passion for whatever profession they choose. On the plane, a pilot spoke to the children about career choices and enjoying what you do, saying that he "loved coming to work."

In summary, words cannot express how valuable this program was to our students. I was especially impressed with the fact that all of those people who gave us their valuable time *did it without pay and on their own time.* None of the participants had any children in our school and none lived in the community. Some presenters had to drive over one hour to get to our school for their presentation. Some did it after working all night, and some did it before going into work. This was truly a community service project and they expected nothing in return. If you have an airlines newspaper, an article referencing this eight-week course would, I am sure, be most refreshing to the airline's employees.

While the children wrote thank you notes to all of the participants, please share our sincere thanks and appreciation for an experience that will be with the children for the rest of their lives.

Sincerely,
L.D.M.
Media, Pennsylvania

We Never Give Up

The "Spirit of Greatness" at American? I'll tell you what it's about—it's never giving up when one of our passengers needs help. Even if it means dismantling a plane!

I worked in Consumer Relations for 14 years and tackled a lot of problems. One day, I received a frantic call from a lady who had lost her wedding ring during a flight. She was seated by a window, and had dropped the ring into a crevice between the wall and the floor. The lady was especially distraught because the ring had been copied for her from the design for Princess Diana's engagement ring.

To begin the search, I got the tail number of the aircraft, then called our maintenance base in Tulsa to see when the plane was next scheduled for a major service. The foreman I talked with in Tulsa had his doubts about retrieving the ring, but when I explained to him how special the ring was, and how important it was to the passenger, he thought there was one mechanic that might be able to recover the ring. When the plane arrived in Tulsa a few months later for its scheduled maintenance, the check list also included, "Find the ring under seat 22A!" After taking the side panels off the belly of the plane, our mechanic reached down into the nuts and bolts of the belly and found the sparkling, elusive ring as good as new. Even though it took us a couple of months, we had one excited passenger when I called to tell her we had found the ring.

Mary Lou Gay
Retired Service Representative
Consumer Relations
Headquarters

Quick Thinking

In the late 1960's, our New York sales office sold a 707 charter to Mr. Harold Geneen, then chairman of ITT, for an executive meeting in London. We had 28 of the most senior ITT executives all on one plane, all at the same time. The charter was the first American Airlines flight to London for about 20 years. The ultra-First Class service contained the finest wines, thousands of dollars in gourmet meals, five movies and the best cigars. Our chief pilot was captain, our executive chef from the general office worked the galley, and we had a doctor, nurse, and a security guard onboard. Our New York sales office even sent a senior representative to coordinate all the details. Every detail was taken into consideration, or so we thought.

When we landed at London Gatwick, we taxied to the terminal and our captain asked Ground Control for fuel. We were horrified when a disturbed looking Exxon supervisor came onboard and informed us that because we had forgotten to obtain a credit standing for Exxon in Europe, they would not fuel our plane. In the face of a complete disaster with ITT, our sales rep calmly took out his personal automobile Exxon credit card, studied the back (which contained no credit limit), handed the card to the fueling supervisor and said, "Fill it up."

Exxon billed the personal card for more than $10,000 and our representative saved the day. I think this is the stuff that makes American great.

Kay Muller
Flight Attendant
Dallas/Fort Worth

Heroic Team

In 1972, Captain Bryce McCormick, First Officer Paige Whitney, Flight Engineer Clay Burk, and their passengers, took off from Detroit's Metropolitan Airport flying a DC-10 (ship #103).

Shortly after take-off, a rear cargo door blew off the plane (due to a faulty locking mechanism design) and the resulting rapid decompression caused the passenger cabin floor to collapse into the cargo hold. The control cables running beneath the floor to the #2 engine, the rudder, and the elevator, were cut or jammed. This left them with no pitch or turn control.

The crew found they still had use of the ailerons which gave them only roll control. While advancing the throttle, Captain McCormick noticed the plane nose pitched up. This discovery led McCormick and Whitney to realize they could use asymmetrical thrust to maneuver the aircraft. That is, by reducing the amount of thrust from the right wing engine and increasing the thrust on the left wing engine, they were able to turn left. Similarly, they could reverse the process for a right turn. By pulling the power on both, they could lower the nose. Although this maneuver was something they had tried in the simulator at the Flight Academy during initial training, there were, at the time, no official technical procedures for this type of emergency.

When the incident occurred, the crew had no idea what had happened. Had they hit another aircraft? Had the #2 engine in the tail exploded? It wasn't until the #1 flight attendant described the hole in the side of the airplane that they realized where and how badly the plane was actually damaged.

The alternate landing sites the crew had been considering were quickly dismissed with the news from the flight attendant. The crew decided they had to return to Detroit. By making long slow turns they were able to return for the emergency landing.

Because of the damage, the crew was unable to use the brakes, and fearing that the nose landing gear wheel would be turned and locked, as was the rudder, the crew prepared to steer and stop the aircraft during landing using the same thing that had flown them back to the airport—asymmetrical thrust.

Upon touch-down, instead of veering to the left as expected, they drifted to the right—directly towards the fire station at the airport! First Officer Whitney quickly adjusted the thrust reversers to straighten out the aircraft and begin its correction back toward the center line. When the aircraft came to a final stop, its left main gear and nose gear were back on the concrete. As it turned out, departing the runway surface had actually helped them come to a safe stop because the gear sank into the soft ground.

As soon as the aircraft came to rest, Captain McCormick gave the signal to his flight attendants to begin the emergency evacuation. All 57 passengers and 11 crew had been returned safely.

Soon after the landing, it was discovered that one of the flight attendants, Bea Donovan, had been seated where the floor collapsed. When the floor fell into the cargo area, it sloped like a ramp toward the gaping hole where the cargo door had once been. Miraculously, a refreshment bar in the rear passenger area had fallen over with the slanted floor and caught Ms. Donovan's legs, preventing her from sliding out of the airplane fully conscious.

American Airlines awarded Captain McCormick and his crew the "Distinguished Service" award—the single highest honor given by American Airlines to any of its employees.

Mark Terpening
Program Developer
Flight Training

We Do Whatever It Takes

Last year I was traveling on American while on vacation from Trinidad to San Juan, Puerto Rico. I was seated next to an elderly woman who was traveling alone and I noticed she was having difficulty breathing. She also could barely talk.

Even though I work in Marketing, not in Passenger Service, I realized that she was one of our customers, and I had to assist her.

I helped her lift her cup, and I spoon fed her meal to her. When we landed in San Juan, she was escorted off the flight in a wheelchair, but she gave me a big hug and a smile. We both had a wonderful flight.

Our flight attendant thanked me for being a part of their crew, but I've always known that being a part of American means doing whatever it takes to help.

Maureen Gallagher
Director of Marketing
AMR Investments
Dallas/Fort Worth

"That's Why I ALWAYS Fly American"

Following an announcement that several DFW-bound flights had been diverted to Austin due to bad weather, a young woman waiting at the gate burst into tears. Frantic and alarmed, she asked for my help. "My grandmother is on that flight. She's 90 years old, completely blind, and very hard of hearing! She also has a heart condition—what if something's happened to her? She'll be confused. She won't understand!" I assured her that I knew her grandmother would be well taken care of by our people in Austin, but that we would find her, and make certain she was all right.

I called Austin and spoke with several gate agents. We finally located her grandmother, who had been taken to a hotel in Austin, courtesy of American Airlines. She was having dinner in her room and seemed to be having a wonderful time. When her granddaughter got on the phone sounding frazzled but relieved, the grandmother was surprised at the young woman's distress. She said, "Honey, what were you worried about? Everything's been taken care of. Don't you know that's why I ALWAYS fly American Airlines! American is like family, they take care of you until you get there!" The relieved granddaughter shared with me what her grandmother had said and thanked me for my help. I couldn't have been paid a higher compliment.

Beverly Moncrief
International Reservations
Dallas/Fort Worth

Our Littlest Customers

On a return business trip from Phoenix to Dallas/Fort Worth, I observed a family in distress at the security checkpoint.

The mom and dad had bought their five-year-old son two shiny play pistols while on vacation in an old ghost town. The security agent had properly confiscated the guns and the little boy was just shattered.

I sat two rows behind the family and the boy sobbed all the way home. I have three children of my own and could relate to his broken heart. I also didn't want him to remember his vacation on American as something less than it could be, so I asked our flight attendant to get me his name and address.

When we landed, I immediately called the Phoenix station manager and his assistant walked down to Security, obtained the toy guns and overnighted them to my home. I, in turn, overnighted them to the little boy's home.

I received a wonderful letter of thanks from the family via my supervisor and an even more rewarding hand drawn picture of thanks from the boy. Best of all, the next time this family buys an airline ticket, I'll bet it's on our airline.

Sherri Garroutte
Senior Avionics Technical Representative
Tulsa

Prepared for Anything

My wife is an international flight attendant based in San Francisco. She's been with American for more than 18 years, is purser qualified, and generally flies San Jose-Tokyo. I know how special she is, but I doubt many people know of her unique talent.

While jogging during a Tokyo layover, she ran past a local farm and noticed a Japanese fellow in some distress, trying to deal with a cow in labor. Lyn spent some of her childhood on a ranch and is a 4-H veteran. Although there was a language barrier, Lyn's offer of help was gratefully accepted. The "farmer" turned out to be a greatly alarmed caretaker, with no idea of how to help the cow. He did, however, have a cell phone and called the owner of the cow while Lyn diagnosed the problem. The owner asked to speak to Lyn who, by that time, had determined that the cow was having a breech birth. The owner, who spoke broken English, asked Lyn for help. The caretaker helped Lyn as best he could, and with a little maneuvering, she was able to re-position the calf in the canal so that the birth was normal. As the birth progressed, the caretaker remained on the phone, apparently giving the farmer a blow-by-blow description of Lyn's efforts. When it was over and the calf was birthed successfully, the farmer thanked her profusely.

A crew from a competing airline came by and were pretty darned impressed. Everyone agreed training class prepares you for a lot of things, but a cow in labor is not one of them! Several trips later, Lyn stopped by to check out the calf, which had been named after Lyn's crew captain, and had her picture taken with it and the caretaker. Last we heard, mother and baby were doing fine.

Chuck Smith
Husband of Flight Attendant
San Francisco

Listening Can Make a Difference

When I was a cargo agent, I would meet inbound and out-bound flights on a regular basis. One day, as I arrived at the gate, a weary businessman approached me. Obviously, he could see from my uniform that I worked for American. He looked very angry—just about ready to explode. Figuring he was about to ask me a question, I told him, "I will help if I can, but I'm from Cargo." He then said, "You work for American Airlines, don't you?" "Yes," I said. For the next four or five minutes, he proceeded to rant about the flight being overbooked and how he'd been inconvenienced. As I was wondering what I might do for him, and preparing an apology in my head, he stopped and said, "Thank you." I asked why he was thanking me, since I hadn't done anything. Then he said, "I just had to get it off my chest, and you listened. Thanks." He said nothing else. Seeming a little happier, he just walked away.

It was a good lesson. Sometimes, listening makes all the difference in the world, and at American, we're good listeners, no matter what department we work in. He also made me realize that I am American Airlines!

Ronald J. Boerst
Retired Operations Agent
Chicago-O'Hare

A Welcome Sight

At Chicago-O'Hare's international arrivals area, we sometimes see more than 1,000 people within 90 minutes as they re-check their luggage after customs inspection.

Unfortunately, you sometimes feel like you are doing little more than herding them through, and you wonder how well you're doing your job.

Once in a while, however, something will happen that will give you a clue.

Recently, in the middle of a crowd of harried passengers, an elderly woman peered at me strangely as she passed her luggage. She called out to her friend, "Come here and look at this!" Now I was really curious, and a bit self-conscious. Did I have my blouse on backwards?

They both stood there and stared at me for a moment. Then the woman exclaimed, "Isn't that beautiful? A smile!" She explained that, after ten days in another country, where she never saw anyone smile, mine was the first she had seen, and it was a welcome sight, indeed.

I didn't even realize that I was smiling. The American Airlines philosophy of treating the customer pleasantly had become second nature to me—and it was really paying off!

Miriam Mayer-Mader
International Arrivals Agent
Chicago-O'Hare

Initiative

Self-motivation is important in any job, but it's something they really stress at American Airlines. If you care to make a difference, then you can make a difference. Here's what I mean: I happened to be in one of the terminal restrooms when a nicely dressed woman with two young girls came in. The restroom was cleaned by an outside company, not by American, and it wasn't in the best condition. Within a few seconds, the girls exclaimed loudly to their mother, "This airline has the worst bathroom ever." And with that, they dashed out of the restroom.

This incident really bothered me. It made me realize that the image of American Airlines really starts from the moment a passenger enters the terminal, not simply after they've boarded the plane. So I wrote a note to both the general manager and the facilities manager at the airport, relaying to them what I had just witnessed, and made suggestions for improvements. I unofficially became the ad hoc Ambassador of Public Facilities. The reaction from both managers was positive and rapid, and the facilities improved noticeably.

Now I speak up all the time, because I am American Airlines.

Monika Lunser
Staff Assistant, Flight Service
New York-Kennedy

Fearful Flyer Takes to the Air

Many years ago, one of our ticket agents in Buffalo was making a reservation for a gentleman who had an unnerving experience on another airline and was now fearful of flying. Our agent was alert enough to remember a similar situation in which Cherrie Webber, a customer service manager, helped a passenger overcome his fear of flying. Our agent called upon Cherrie again.

Every Saturday morning for several months, Cherrie sat with the gentleman on an empty plane, talking him through the flight procedure. They sat in each seat until he found one in which he was comfortable enough to overcome his fear of flying and take his trip. After many visits to the airport, and with Cherrie's assistance, he was finally ready to venture out on his own from Buffalo to Chicago and then on to Las Vegas. Cherrie reassured the man that if at any point during his trip he felt he could not continue, she would fly out to meet him and accompany him on the return.

The gentleman called her from each leg of the trip, thrilled with his progress—victorious by the time he reached Las Vegas! Cherrie's outstanding patience and compassion not only won American the gentleman's loyalty, but the loyalty of his friends.

Ann Dudley
Manager, Passenger Service
Dallas/Fort Worth

Trust In American Airlines

Dear American,

I was at the AA office at the Antigua airport. A woman at the counter was attempting to purchase a ticket to Vermont because her daughter had died suddenly.

Her credit-card company declined authorization, and she didn't have another way to purchase the needed ticket.

Boston-based Captain David Hallett heard her predicament and offered to pay for the ticket out of his own pocket.

This was an incredibly generous and caring gesture on the part of Captain Hallett. He didn't know if he'd be reimbursed for this ticket. All he knew was that an American Airlines customer was in trouble and he could help.

I'm glad that I was present because it reaffirmed my faith and trust in American Airlines.

R.B.
Antigua

Excerpts from *Flagship News*, July 4, 1994

He Can Fly My Airplane Anytime

I just completed a trip with Captain Stuart Kingman, who lives on a mountain ridge in Morgan Hill, south of the San Jose airport. Last month, with all the El Niño problems impacting our crews, Captain Kingman was on reserve and received an urgent call to be at the airport "now" to cover another crew problem.

He rushed to get ready and started down the mountain toward the airport. Rounding the last curve, he discovered that a major mudslide had closed the mountain road right in front of him.

Rather than fail to cover his flight, Captain Kingman arranged for his brother-in-law to meet him on the other side of the mountain. Captain Kingman changed into his "grubby' clothes and hiking boots, threw his uniform into a back pack and hiked over the mudslide to connect with his brother-in-law.

He made it to the airport in time for the trip. If you've ever heard the expression, "He's the guy you call at 3:00 in the morning when you get a flat tire," well, I think they are talking about Stu Kingman.

Robert Dunning
First Officer
San Jose

A Pick-Up at a Bad Time

I think that a company that recognizes and rewards its employees understands the best way to build respect and loyalty.

In March 1996, I submitted a suggestion to combine all of our American Eagle freight shipping onto one system to the American Airlines "IdeAAs In Action" program. What I thought was a rather simple and modest proposal ended up saving the company almost $650,000 annually.

In June 1997, my husband died and I entered a very low point in my life. I became extremely lonely, bills mounted, and the uncertainty of what the future would hold for a single parent with a six-year-old was awful.

It's no wonder that I had forgotten all about my suggestion.

Then, about a month after my husband's death, I received a call from American Airlines that I had been awarded $25,000 for my suggestion! There were other perks, too: a special trip to Los Angeles, free Coach travel for a year, and some wonderful memories of lots of caring people at a time when it was so important to me.

American was there for me when I really needed them. Thank you.

Suzanna Eads
Inventory Analyst
Miami

Positive Impact

What I find really great about American Airlines is that every employee has the ability to impact positively the growth of our company, no matter what their job title is.

Recently, as I was walking through the terminal on my way home, I recognized Florida's senator, Bob Graham, who had just arrived. No one from Special Services was at the gate, so I walked over and greeted him on behalf of American Airlines. I asked if he had a pleasant flight, and if he needed any further assistance. He was quite impressed that a fleet service clerk would take the time to assist him. He was certainly kind enough to write me the attached letter, which I was very pleased to receive.

United States Senate

September, 15 1997

Dear Kevin,

It was a pleasure seeing you at the Miami International Airport on September 5, 1997. I am convinced that if you spent enough time there, you would eventually meet all of your lifetime acquaintances and a high percentage of the human population.

Kevin, thank you for your gracious service at the Miami airport. Probably more people get their first impression of our community and state there than at any other place in Florida. I appreciate your providing them with such a positive introduction.

I appreciate your kind remarks, I will strive to continue to justify your confidence.

Sincerely,
Bob Graham
United States Senator

Kevin Aronoff
Fleet Service Clerk, Baggage Room
Miami

Why We Choose American

Once, when I was a supervisor at JFK Airport, we were requested to pre-board a totally disabled passenger in a motorized wheelchair.

The woman was a quadriplegic and very large. It was immediately apparent that even with the assistance of my lead agent and her traveling companion, we would not be able to board this passenger with the dignity and grace we had been trained to provide in these situations.

I immediately contacted our supervisor in line cargo, Jim Wilson, and after explaining the situation, asked him for his assistance. Without a moment's hesitation, Jim arrived with his crew and within minutes, we had the passenger onboard and comfortably seated without stress or incident. Mr. Wilson and his crew wished her a pleasant flight, and thanked her for flying American. The teamwork and cooperation between many departments is what American Airlines is all about. What has stuck in my mind all these years is the comment her traveling companion made to me as I wished them a bon voyage: "Thank you. *This* is why we choose American Airlines."

Penney Herrel-McCormick
Retired Passenger Service Supervisor
New York-Kennedy

A Little Extra Effort Goes a Long Way

In the mailroom, from time to time, we come across mail that was sent to American by accident. Most of the mail we handle is nothing unusual—business letters, bills, junk mail. But one day we found some very special cargo in the misdirected mail. There was a birthday card with a check enclosed from a grandmother to her grandson.

Unfortunately, the envelope was damaged and the address of the grandson was missing. Luckily, grandma's address was on the check. We contacted information and were able to find her number. A call was placed to grandma to tell her what had happened. She gave us the grandson's address and was thrilled that we took the time to help. We quickly re-addressed the letter, stamped it, and sent it on its way—arriving in time for the grandson's birthday. I'm proud to work for American Airlines, where people will do things like this for someone they don't even know.

> Marilyn Hinds
> AAdvantage Mail Clerk
> Headquarters

Two for the Price of One

In 1993, American Airlines' Consumer Relations department received two letters in the same envelope. One was from the president of a large corporation:

Ms. Jan Ferguson
American Airlines
Consumer Relations

Dear Ms. Ferguson,

Far too seldom do we take the time to make mention of someone who does an outstanding job. We are all too quick to criticize when things do not go well but just fail to note good service.

I am an AAdvantage Gold member and have occasion to fly in and out of Little Rock on many trips. Often, I am fortunate enough to have your Donna Norman tend to my seat assignments. Ms. Norman does her job in a very professional, friendly manner. She should be commended for always doing an outstanding job.

C.C.
President

The second letter was from Mr. C's assistant who, in preparing his letter, realized she was writing to the same employee who had once helped her:

Ms. Ferguson,

I work as Mr. C's personal assistant. When he gave me the enclosed letter to mail to you, I noticed the name Donna Norman. I too, had the pleasure of meeting Ms. Norman. My experience occurred on August 18, 1991—two years ago. My husband and I were leaving on our honeymoon to Cancun, Mexico. The travel agent we used failed to advise us of a need for proof of citizenship. We found out at the airport that this information was incorrect. We were in a panic and didn't think we would be able to go on our honeymoon. Our tickets were non-refundable, we left our car at the hotel and took a shuttle to the airport, and we both lived at least 45 minutes form the airport. Donna saved the day. She offered us the use of her personal car to go home and get our birth certificates. I was able to drive very fast to our homes, pick up both birth certificates and get back to the airport. Donna had put us on another flight and we made our connection to Dallas with seconds to spare.

Donna certainly went above and beyond the call of duty when it came to helping two complete strangers. We will be forever in debt to her. If we had been flying another airline or had a different agent helping us, I'm sure the outcome of our trip would have been very different.

If employees with your company receive promotions, raises or bonuses based on attitude and service, Donna

absolutely deserves one. This was the most positive experience I have ever had with any airline. My husband
and I tell this story all the time. We also recommend to
all our friends and family to fly American Airlines and
ask for Donna. I know Donna will probably not remember us because I'm sure we are just two of many
people she gives "special treatment" to each day, however, I would appreciate it if you would send her my best
regards.

Sincerely,
C.C.
Assistant to Mr. C.

Greg Klein
General Manager
Little Rock

It Doesn't Matter What Color Shirt You Wear

David Thoren, a fellow team member who works in Ramp Services, recently found a checkbook, with credit cards and other valuables, belonging to an arriving passenger.

David took the time to track down the passenger and return his checkbook and valuables. We received a wonderful letter from him which ended with, "People like David Thoren are an important reason why I fly American Airlines."

I'm also proud of people like David, who, although they don't work directly in Passenger Service, recognize that all American employees are responsible for helping our customers, regardless of what color shirt they wear to work that day—blue or white!

Ricardo L. Baquero
Manager, Line Cargo
Miami

Shepherd One

In 1992 American Airlines was awarded the right to transport the pope and his party from the U.S. back to Rome. Thus began a year long preparation that included the construction of a special bed for the pope onboard the plane.

It was already dark in Denver at 8:45 p.m. on Sunday, August 15, 1993, when Pope John Paul II climbed the stairs leading to an American Airlines Boeing 767-300ER designated "Shepherd One." It was the end of the pontiff's historic visit to the United States and the end of World Youth Day, a gathering of hundreds of thousands of young Catholics. But for AA employees, it was the beginning of an unprecedented event—the first time American Airlines had flown the pontiff.

Nearly 11 hours and 5,800 miles later, the plane landed in Rome, where the pope was greeted with military fanfare and a red carpet. Roberto Antonucci, American's general manager at Milan, was among the greeters when the plane landed at Rome's Ciampino Airport. "I introduced myself," said Antonucci, "then the pope smiled and said, 'American Airlines—good service.' "

Providing that service was a cockpit crew of five headed by Captain Lee Schumacher and an 11-member cabin crew, including May Lannes, who served the pope in First Class. "It was awesome," Schumacher said. "He invited every member of the crew to sit down with him in First Class." Schumacher praised cabin crew members, who received many compliments from the passengers, "They were absolutely stunning—absolutely fantastic."

Excerpts from *Flagship News,* August 23, 1993

Isn't That Really What My Job Is About?

My team is responsible for the training and development of American Airlines employees in the MCLA (Miami/Caribbean/Latin American) division. Recently, I felt our employees needed additional training in the use of our various computer systems. Since we did not have a budget for this additional training, I used my vacation time to travel throughout my division.

I knew the immediate sacrifice on my part would not only help to make another employee's job a little easier, but in the long run would make American Airlines a stronger company for the passengers we are here to serve—and isn't that really what my job is about?

K. Sergio
Staff Assistant
Learning & Development
Miami

We Do What Has To Be Done

About a year ago, on a very windy day, the crew I was working with spotted a cart full of mail at another gate being pushed by the wind straight across the field on a direct collision course with a United flight that was backing out. Without a word, our entire crew all broke into a run—catching the cart just in time. I think it's things like this that make our company great—everyone taking responsibility to see that things go right. I went home that night and I felt really good about my crew.

Andre Wayne Malloy
Fleet Service Clerk
New York-LaGuardia

Yo Hablo Español

As a 767 captain, I strongly believe that it is very important to good customer relations that we communicate to our passengers in their own language whenever possible. As a result, I've been struggling to master my PA's from the cockpit in Spanish. Recently a passenger sent the enclosed note (written on a napkin) to the cockpit. This note really made my day and makes the extra work to learn Spanish so worthwhile. It is a better testimony to my belief than anything I could write:

Cap'n:

Your Spanish rendition of the flight-facts announcement was nothing short of a bravura performance. Bravo to you!! It was so gratifying to hear a gringo trying to communicate with us. One of the most refreshing experiences in 30 years of coming back to my "tierra" (I'm a Peruvian-born U.S. citizen). Keep it up amigo and we'll keep flying American.

A.S.N.

Mark Z. Connell
Captain
Miami

Tony—Wherever You Are, Thank You.

A while ago (I'm not going to date myself!), we taxied into Tucson, Arizona, and were met by our mechanic. He informed us that our brand new DC-6 had to undergo a "mandatory engine inspection." It seemed another DC-6, also equipped with special new propellers, had experienced a propeller failure, which tore the entire engine from the plane. In an amazing display of emergency flying, the pilot of that aircraft landed safely. A subsequent search of the Rocky Mountains flight path uncovered the ripped-out engine with its broken propeller hub—thus the mandatory inspection. We informed our passengers of exactly what was happening and why. No one objected.

A workstand was pulled into place and each engine was washed and cleaned thoroughly with solvent. No crack appeared. The engines were then run up through full range. We shut down and our mechanic again re-checked each engine. Our mechanic was now inspecting the completely clean hubs for the hairline tell-tale track of grease that identified a crack. Since our DC-6 was brand new we didn't expect any problems. I'll always remember him calling to the cockpit: "#1 L/H outboard prop hub clean," "#2 L/H inboard prop hub clean," "#4 R/H outboard prop hub clean." We started working on our departure plan—only one engine left to check. We'd be on our way to Los Angeles in a few moments. Suddenly, we saw the mechanic signal to us to come out to his workstand.

There it was, the faint grease line; it had gone nearly completely around the rear side of the last hub to check.

One good bump and our #3 engine would have probably fallen off the wing.

I have never forgotten this incident. The persistence, diligence and professionalism of our people, in all probability, had saved my crew and all our passengers from a very dangerous situation.

The mechanic, later, flight engineer, was Tony Erkeneff and I will always be thankful to him. Perhaps if this letter gets published he will know how much we appreciate him.

J.S. Brattain
Retired Flight Engineer
Los Angeles

Our Contribution to Medical Science

Most of us think of airline travel as a way to do business or go on vacation, but that's not always the case. From the summer of 1916 until 1955, a vicious killer virus called polio killed, crippled or maimed untold numbers of children and some adults, including President Roosevelt. As the disease went unchecked, the country was brought to its knees. Then in 1955, two scientists, Jonas Salk and Albert Sabin, finally developed a vaccine.

The race was on to vaccinate every child in America. Live Rhesus monkeys were used in the production of the vaccine. This meant shipping thousands of monkeys from Africa to Idlewild (now JFK) Airport, then shuttling via truck to La Guardia for a connection to an American Airlines freighter to Detroit, the location of the vaccine lab.

By the time the monkeys reached New York, they were in anything but prime condition. The stench from the crates was horrendous, and many of the animals were sick or had died.

After the first shipment was on its way to Detroit, most of the American personnel—airport employees, truck drivers, even the freighter flight crew—voiced their objections, insisting the cargo was unacceptable for carriage and should be refused in the future. That's when we learned that no one had told most of our employees about the critical purpose of these shipments. Management quickly called a meeting to explain the shipments.

And that's when the mettle of American Airlines employees emerged. Once everyone understood the importance of the shipments, we all agreed that these shipments would be handled expeditiously. Our people even made valuable suggestions to fix some of the shipping problems and most of them were accepted.

Over the years, the personnel at La Guardia accepted thousands of monkeys for hundreds of air freighter flights. They were proud to be an important part of the vaccination program to eliminate the source of polio.

The moral of this story is that when a humanitarian endeavor is recognized, AA personnel will overcome all obstacles, put up with any inconvenience, and go above and beyond the call of duty to accomplish their goals.

Eugene McCabe
Retired Chief Agent, Freight Control
New York-LaGuardia

We Have a "Saint" in Little Rock

On March 22, 1996, a businesswoman flew from Philadelphia to Dallas/Forth Worth, and then on to a business meeting in Little Rock, Arkansas. Her schedule was hectic with tight connections. Upon arrival in Little Rock she was to rent a car, drive 25 miles to visit an important client, and then immediately drive back to catch her flight to Palm Springs the same day.

When she landed in Little Rock, she was paged to see an American agent. The agent informed her that she had dropped her wallet while connecting in Dallas/Fort Worth, and that it had been found by American personnel who had traced her movements to Little Rock. The wallet was being sent in care of the crew on the next inbound flight.

The woman, realizing she had no money, no credit cards, no driver's license and a very tight schedule, became extremely upset. She tried to persuade the auto rental company to rent her a car, but failed. When she returned to the gate to verify with the agent, Mrs. Angie New, when her wallet would arrive, she discovered it would arrive too late for her to visit her client and make her Palm Springs departure. It appeared her entire trip to Little Rock was wasted, that is, until Mrs. New turned to the very frustrated woman and said, "Why don't you just borrow my car?" The woman thought Mrs. New must be teasing. Mrs. New took a 15-minute coffee break, walked the woman to her car, gave her directions, her cellular phone, and her car keys.

On her return to the airport the woman's wallet had arrived and she was able to make her Palm Springs departure.

The grateful customer wrote to Mr. Carty, then our president, and said, "American Airlines should feel privileged to have Angie New as an employee. She is rare in today's society. As a very frequent traveler, I cannot express how wonderful it is to know I have a friend at American Airlines and a 'saint' living in Little Rock, Arkansas."

Mrs. New received a "Customer Comes First" award and wristwatch for her outstanding service. We are proud to call Mrs. New our colleague.

Greg Klein
General Manager
Little Rock

It's Important to Resolve Problems, Too

Our Boston sales representative, Kathy Bagley, was recently asked to provide assistance to a severely disabled boy traveling with his family to the Caribbean. The boy required the use of a custom-designed wheelchair and special handling at all airports.

Their trip was highly successful. However, the wheelchair was badly damaged on the return trip and could not be fixed. This chair was critical to the boy's mobility, because it was automated to help him move his arms as well.

All of us know that there are times when things don't always go as planned. This was one of those times. However, what's great about American Airlines is that we have the people and the systems in place not only to deal with positive transactions, but the negative ones as well.

Kathy contacted the manufacturer of the custom wheelchair in New Hampshire and discovered the replacement cost was $25,000. She then reviewed the incident with the appropriate insurance people at corporate headquarters and received approval to immediately issue an overnight check for $25,000 to the manufacturer. The new chair was delivered to the family the next day.

American Airlines prides itself on perfection. In our business, we have no margin for error. The measure of a company is not always how well things work, but how well the company resolves problems when they occur.

As a zone sales manager, I was so proud of the dedication and ability that Kathy Bagley demonstrated in resolving the wheelchair incident. I am equally proud that my company as a whole supported Kathy and her effort to help our passenger.

Carl Wimmer
Zone Sales Manger
Boston

Next Stop, Outer Space

I'll never forget the first space shuttle flights. NASA had leased one of our 747s to transport the shuttle between Florida and Edwards Air Force Base in California.

NASA selected our maintenance people to be stationed at Edwards, and I was very fortunate to be cleared to watch from a vehicle on the runway, as the shuttle landed, piggy-backed atop our 747.

American Airlines made a major contribution to our space program, and I'm very honored to have been a part of this effort.

Sharon Casler
Retired Executive Secretary
Aircraft Maintenance
Los Angeles

A Special Thank You

We treat all of our customers the same at American Airlines, but every once in a while we find one that stands out and is more memorable than others. In 1989 we received the following letter:

September 5, 1989

Ms. Sandra Nunnally
General Manager
American Airlines
Little Rock, AR 72202

Dear Ms. Nunnally:

I want to commend Donna Norman and Lorraine Maxwell, two American Airlines employees at the Little Rock airport, for their positive attitude and "grace under pressure." On August 3, 1989, my daughter and I were waiting for your early flight to Dallas/Fort Worth to connect with one of your flights to Honolulu. When the flight had to be delayed because of mechanical reasons, I was among the many passengers Ms. Norman and Ms. Maxwell helped. They were both calm and reassuring, which helped keep all the travelers optimistic that we would all be well taken care of on American Airlines.

I travel a great deal and have become discouraged recently by the blank faces and unhelpful attitudes of too many airline employees. It was a pleasure, even in the midst of disappointment, to run across two who are among the best I have ever seen.

By copy of this letter, I am advising both Ms. Norman and Ms. Maxwell how one grateful passenger feels about them. Thanks.

Sincerely yours,
Hilary Rodham Clinton

Greg Klein
General Manager
Little Rock

Our Customers Win Also

After my initial training as a 727 flight engineer at Dallas/Fort Worth, I was assigned to La Guardia Airport in New York City.

Having preconceived ideas about "cold and unfriendly New Yorkers," I was totally blown away by how friendly and helpful the people at American Airlines were. Everyone I met—from the chief pilot to the flight administrator to the crew administration—told me they were glad to have me onboard and that I should ask for help if I had any problem.

I thought, "If this friendly attitude exists amongst the employees, surely our customers are the real winners." Through the years, my initial thoughts have been reinforced time and time again.

The people at American Airlines and their positive attitude make me proud that I had the opportunity to be one of the elements that makes a company great—its people.

Ted D. Barker
Retired First Officer
Los Angeles

Wow! John Wayne

I was the acting chief agent on the ramp in Buffalo many years ago.

John Wayne was booked on a flight to La Guardia and it was getting very close to departure time. Soon we were ready to go, but still no "Duke." We called his hotel and they said his limo was on the way.

My ramp agent working the flight didn't want the delay and went ahead and booked Mr. Wayne on a later flight.

I thought about it and said, "Let's wait." About a minute later the limo arrived. We quickly checked in "the Duke." Our fleet service clerks were waiting and his luggage was on the plane in seconds.

As we boarded the plane, John Wayne knew we did the right thing for him. He smiled and gave us a "thanks." We ended up only a few minutes late, but we were glad we held the flight. And when he walked onboard, so were our passengers—"Wow, we flew with John Wayne."

G.E. Merryman
Retired Flight Dispatcher
Systems Operations Control

The Right Man in the Right Job

I met C.R. Smith in North Africa while in the Air Transport Command during WWII, and through him was introduced to an American Airlines executive who suggested I go to work for American Airlines after the war. I started with American Overseas Airlines in January 1946, and after three years in Europe, returned to American in Dallas in 1949. C.R. was a frequent visitor to Texas, and because of our WWII connection, we conversed often. His strong personality and commitment to the highest standard of service permeated the whole organization.

In 1966, American re-organized, and I was offered a position in Customer Service at Braniff by Eddie Acker, their president. I stayed at Braniff until they went out of business in 1982. I had made so many senior friends in the Texas business community that a number of them called Bob Crandall to recommend American rehire me. Mr. Crandall didn't know me, but he took a chance, and I rejoined American. I stayed with American until December 1996, and retired as manager of Special Services in Dallas.

Shortly after I retired, American held a luncheon in my honor and many of my customers came from all over to join me. I was so proud that so many civic leaders from Fort Worth and Dallas came. Don Meredith, the football star, came in from Santa Fe; Dolly Parton flew in from Nashville; and Larry Hagman came from California. Ann Richards, former governor of Texas, also attended. Even Al Casey, American's former chairman, came along with just about everyone from corporate headquarters. Father

Gilbert Graham of Texas delivered the invocation at our luncheon and said of me, "Many of us are square pegs in round holes. Not so, Walter Henry Hagan. He was the right man in the right place at the right time."

I've thought about my life at American a lot. My job was to make sure important customers had a good experience on American Airlines. I did my job well, but only because everyone else in our company ensured that the product I had to offer was the best in the business.

Walter Hagan
Retired Manager of Special Services
Dallas/Fort Worth

Our Top Priority

After 34 years with American Airlines, you would think I would have many reasons why American is great. I could give you lots of reasons why it is a good place to work, and why it's a wonderful airline, but I've only got a single word for why American is *great*—safety.

Safety on the ground and in the air is *everyone's* first priority at American. It gives our customers confidence and it gives me lots of pride.

David Nazar
Fleet Service
San Jose

One of Those Days

The Syracuse airport terminal at 1 a.m. was silent and empty on a snowy winter weeknight in1962. I was on duty as a ticket agent, which included responsibility for lost and found problems. I had just closed down the ticket counter. American's last flight, an Electra from Chicago, had arrived an hour earlier. Certainly by this time, all the passengers had their baggage and were on their way.

Slowly walking towards our ticket counter was a man carrying a briefcase and looking confused. He approached me and calmly said he had a problem. (I noticed also he smelled very bad). He said, "I left Los Angeles this morning on TWA and had to hurry at Chicago to connect with American's flight to Syracuse. Arriving here for the first time, I had this urgent need to use the men's room. I followed the signs and found the men's room. As I sat on the commode, I flushed the toilet and the water backed up, forcing me quickly off the seat. Both my suit and trench coat fell from the door hook to the floor and into the water. Everything was wet, and I had to use the hand air dryer attempting to dry my briefs. When I finally arrived at the baggage claim, I couldn't find my baggage. I need my bag since I have a business meeting at 9:00 a.m. at General Electric. What else can go wrong? Could you help me?"

"Wow," I said. He and I had to be the only ones in the terminal. The last cabs and limos were long gone. I knew, especially because of the smell, that he'd have difficulty being accepted as a hotel guest. So the first thing I needed to do to help his situation was to phone the hotel and inquire about valet service at the same time.

I called the hotel, confirmed his reservation, and after explaining my passenger's problem to the hotel manager, learned that valet service was not available at that time of night. Then, I asked the business traveler, if he could possibly fit into a size 40 dark suit, wear a white shirt (size 15 1/2 by 33), socks, handkerchief and underclothes? His response was a definite "Yes, God Bless!"

I had him wait for me in the terminal while I went to the parking lot, warmed up and brushed snow off my car before picking him up. We proceeded to my home, stopping briefly to pick up the clothes, and then finally headed off to the hotel, arriving about 2:00 a.m.

My next stop was to a familiar bar, for a beer and an attentive bartender.

When I returned for work the next afternoon, I was told to report to the manager's office immediately. After relating the series of events to him, I noticed my clothes, neatly dry cleaned on a tree-rack and an envelope attached to them. (Inside was a $20 bill and a note that read, "Jim, I'll never forget the help and service you provided me. My appointment was a success. And I'll always fly American. I'm heading home now. Many thanks.")

His suitcase arrived on the first morning flight from Chicago. It was never opened while he was in Syracuse.

James J. Korzelius
Retired Senior Cost Accountant
Tulsa

Who Says There's No Santa Claus?

Back in December 1944, I was working right seat (co-pilot) on flights between Mexico and the United States. Our captain received a call from the manager of a small station in Victoria, Mexico, asking for a favor. It seems a package of toys from the States was not going to make it to his town in time for Christmas.

We were asked to pick up the toys, and on our next trip to Mexico City, fly over Victoria and drop the package of toys (which were wrapped in extra packaging to protect them) from the plane.

We picked up the toys and flew south. When we reached Victoria, the captain radioed the manager and told him we were going to drop the toys on the runway. The captain slowed the plane over the runway and told me to push the box of toys out. But I couldn't open the door far enough, so the captain had to make a second run, use the flaps, lower the landing gear and really slow down the aircraft enough so that I could get the door open. It worked! The Victoria manager radioed up that not even one toy was broken.

What made this even more interesting was that we were carrying passengers, and they were aware of what we were going to do. Rather than objecting, they were excited about the whole adventure!

That special bond between American Airlines and its passengers goes back a long way.

G.J. Kahak
Retired Captain, Chief Pilot
Dallas/Fort Worth

Editor's note: We received dozens of printed business cards from retired employees along with their *"A Spirit of Greatness"* submissions. Each card had the American logo, their name, and under their name, the word "retired." One of our editors remarked, "I've never seen anything like this company. These employees are retired, but retirement is totally different to them than it is to employees of other companies." I thought about it for a moment, looked around my office with AA "stuff" hanging on the walls here and there and replied, "You're right, it *is* different."

An Anniversary to Remember

American Airlines
Customer Service Department

To Whom It May Concern,

I'll never forget our 40th wedding anniversary—but not for the reasons you might expect.

My wife and I had planned to celebrate this landmark occasion by taking a cruise. The ship was set to depart at 10 p.m. from San Juan, Puerto Rico. It would be a full day of traveling to get there, starting with a 6:40 a.m. flight out of Sacramento, followed by a connecting flight to San Juan. We had planned for everything—except the fog.

Poor visibility grounded our flight for an hour and a half. With only an hour between flights, the delay would have kept us from making our connection, and worse, from getting to the cruise ship on time—that is, if it weren't for your employee, Candy Tasker.

Somehow, Candy managed to get us on another flight to San Juan that would arrive shortly before our cruise ship's departure. But Candy's diligence did not end there. There was still the issue of our luggage, which was on our originally scheduled flight—now delayed three hours!

Literally, taking us by our hands, my wife practically in tears, Candy escorted us through Security to our new flight. We boarded within minutes of departure. As we sat breathlessly through the take-off, we still were not sure whether our luggage had been transferred. What we also didn't know was that Candy, herself, was moments away from missing her own flight to Little Rock.

We arrived on time in San Juan, and boarded the cruise ship with just ten minutes to spare. To our surprise, our luggage did too. Candy had come through once again! We later found out that Candy had missed her flight to Little Rock because of us. We will always be grateful for the personal attention she gave us.

My wife and I have been on many flights, both foreign and domestic, but have never experienced the level of service Candy Tasker provided. It was truly above and beyond the call of duty. And, because of her, it truly was an anniversary to remember.

Sincerely,
F.B.S.
Grass Valley, California

Saving the Day

Mr. John Capozzi
A Spirit of Greatness

Dear John,

I started with American as a rookie agent in Boston, assigned to the 4 p.m. to midnight shift, in what was then called Lost and Found. At that time, Boston was the predominant airport for most of New England.

After our nonstop flight from Los Angeles arrived, a very nervous and upset man appeared before me stating that his checked luggage was missing. I apologized for this mishap, and started to explain the procedures for lost luggage. He interrupted me and said, "You don't understand, I am conducting a training seminar for 40 of our salespeople in Rhode Island tomorrow morning at 8 a.m., and all my slides and collateral support for the seminar are in those bags." He further stated that all of his company's management would be attending the seminar and the loss of his presentation material would wreck his career.

At that point the only thing I could tell him was that I would do everything within my power to locate the bags. Nevertheless, because we did not have another Los Angeles flight scheduled to arrive in Boston until the next day, I was not optimistic about getting his material to him in time for his seminar.

I also offered to call his supervisor and explain the

situation to him. Although he appreciated my offer, this did nothing to quiet his anxiety, and he left.

I quickly got on the phone to Los Angeles, no luck; they had no record of the bags not connecting on his flight. I sent out a system wide search message explaining the situation—again no luck.

At the completion of my shift (midnight), as I was walking to the employee parking lot, I felt badly for our passenger, so I decided to return to the terminal and check with the other airlines and do a visible check of their baggage rooms. There was absolutely no reason why his bags would have been put on a transfer cart, but as fate would have it, I found the two bags sitting in Delta's bag room. They had been mistakenly put into a transfer pod.

I claimed the two bags, got into my car and drove to Rhode Island, and at 4 a.m. our passenger had his luggage. To this day, I can still see the expression of relief and disbelief on his face.

He wrote a wonderful thank you note to American, which earned me a "Customer Comes First" watch. However, the greatest reward was over the next years. When this customer came to Boston, he made a point of seeking me out to say "hi," and let me know that he was a committed American Airlines customer.

Carter Bibbey

What Would You Do?!

Two vacationers wearing only their bathing suits, were standing in front of Puerto Plata Passenger Service Agent, Nilda Ventura. They had no tickets, no cash, no credit cards, no identification, nothing—except two towels.

The California couple had sailed into the Dominican Republic that morning on a cruise ship and had come ashore for the day. Mixed signals caused the couple to miss their bus back to the ship. After finally flagging down a taxi, they arrived at the pier just in time to watch their ship head out to sea.

Desperate and clad only in bathing suits, the couple persuaded the taxi to take them to the airport to catch a flight to the ship's next port of call. Fortunately, they found Nilda Ventura at the American ticket counter. Nilda arranged hotel accommodations and advanced them $40 to pay for their taxi. Security Agent, John Mancini, personally loaned them another $20. Ventura and Mancini worked well beyond their shift to finalize arrangements for the couple to fly to San Juan the next day to catch their ship. American even provided meal vouchers for the airport cafeteria, since the couple had not eaten anything.

"When it was time for our flight to board, Nilda walked us through immigration, gave us a big hug at the gate and said she was glad to be of help," the grateful gentleman said. "Without the help of Nilda and the wonderful American staff at Puerto Plata Airport, we don't know what we would have done."

Excerpts from *Flagship News*, February 1, 1993

74

Caring for Our Customers

During my 27-year career with American, I received many wonderful customer letters, as well as an "Outstanding Service" award from the Airline Passenger Association, for my contribution to the welfare of airline passengers. I also received a certificate of appreciation from the United States government for my service to basic trainees during my years as a supervisor in El Paso.

However, the most satisfying event occurred while I worked as a reservations agent at what was then Amon Carter Field in Fort Worth. While working the late shift, I received a call from the airport about an elderly woman who had just missed the last flight to California. She had just attended her daughter's funeral and was traveling with her four-month-old granddaughter.

The grandmother was exhausted. She needed a place to stay, diapers and milk. At the time, I had a son only a few months old, so I was completely set up to handle a small child. Since I was about to get off duty, I volunteered to drive to the airport, pick up the grandmother and child, and take them to my home, where my wife and I could bathe and feed the child while the grandmother got some rest. The next morning, we had them on their way to California, well-rested with extra diapers and formula.

Norman Wight
Retired Reservations Agent
Dallas

Every Creature Deserves the Best

When the American Society for the Prevention of Cruelty to Animals (ASPCA) honored American Airlines with its Corporate Citizen Award, it was the first time the nation's oldest humane association had honored an airline for its work with animals.

"American has been a good friend to animals," said Roger Caras, ASPCA president. "By recognizing that traveling pets are precious family members and that every creature deserves safety and reasonable comfort in transport, AA has set a standard in the industry."

American and the ASPCA have teamed up on several projects. The two are best known for rescuing three African lions targeted for death in late 1994. To accommodate the rescue coordinated by the ASPCA and several Texas organizations, American placed a large-body jet on a route typically served by a smaller plane so the animals could travel together safely on the same flight. The lions now live in a sanctuary near Fort Worth. American also serves as the official airline of the Brookfield Zoo in Chicago, the Dallas Zoo and the Metro Zoo in Miami.

On average, American transports more than 270 animals each day, including some of America's most famous animals: Siegfried and Roy's white tigers, Nipper and Chipper (the RCA dogs), Lassie, and Murray of NBC's *"Mad About You."*

In 1995, American Airlines also became the first airline to receive the Animal Welfare Award from the Animal Transportation Association.

Excerpts from *Flagship News,* April 22, 1996

CONFIDENTIAL

I retired in 1986 as a supervisor in Flight Ground Training at our Flight Academy. One of the most interesting highlights of my career came during the spate of airplane hijackings in the early 1970s. It seemed that the more TV coverage that was given to these events, the more the incidents occurred.

American Airlines took a very strong stand to protect its passengers and crews. The news reported that we had arranged for U.S. Marshalls to ride on selected flights—but that was only a small part of a very detailed and highly confidential program. The U.S. Marshalls were actually carefully screened FBI agents. All had previous experience in military flight (mostly in Vietnam). We not only taught them the American Airlines operating procedures, but we also trained them in the simulator to fly and land our equipment in the event that any of our crews became incapacitated.

Neither our passengers nor our crews knew about the level of support we were putting on our flights. But I was really proud of our company during this difficult period in our history.

R.J. "Bob" Kalina
Retired Supervisor of Boeing Equipment
Flight Ground Training
Flight Academy

A Valuable Tip

Flight attendants face many challenges on a daily basis—some big, some small. And sometimes, it's the small efforts that make a big difference to passengers, as noted in a letter of recognition from a grateful passenger. It's the kind of letter that makes your day, if you're an employee, but also offers a valuable tip, if you're a frequent flyer with sinus trouble:

> On a recent flight from Dallas/Fort Worth to San Diego, I experienced severe sinus and ear pain. Chicago-O'Hare-based Charles Glasso helped me with a special remedy I hadn't seen before. He brought me two plastic cups with wet, hot wash cloths inside, and placed the cups over my ears. Within 30 minutes, the pain and congestion were relieved.
>
> His skilled and kind attention changed my flight from a painful to a pleasant experience. I'm writing to recognize an outstanding flight attendant and to thank American for having such highly qualified and professional flight attendants.

Excerpts from *Flagship News*, May 28, 1997

Special Arrangements

Mr. Don Carty
Chairman and CEO
American Airlines

Dear Mr. Carty,

We are writing this letter to make you aware of the exceptional service provided to us by Carole Goldstein.

On Saturday, June 6, 1998, my wife and I were at UC Davis Medical Center in Sacramento, California. Earlier that week, my wife's father experienced end-stage renal disease and came very close to death. He underwent dialysis on Friday and Saturday, and we were told by his doctor that the best time to move him home to Dallas would be that Saturday, June 6. I spent about four hours on the phone trying to schedule a direct flight to Dallas that same day. My wife and I had return tickets with TWA for the following Monday night, but TWA was unwilling to allow us to reschedule or refund our tickets so that we could accompany her father and mother to Dallas on Saturday.

We called Ticket Reservations at American Airlines and were transferred to Carole Goldstein. We informed her that we would be unable to accompany my wife's parents to Dallas that evening because of the circumstances with TWA. We told Carole that we could not afford not to use the TWA tickets and pay an additional $876 each to fly with her parents on American Airlines.

After relating our entire story to Carole, she performed what we consider to be the greatest act of compassion by a representative of a large corporation that we have ever experienced. Carole apologized for the insensitivity of TWA and arranged for all four of us to fly to Dallas together at a greatly reduced rate. But Carole did not stop there. When we informed her that my wife's father would need oxygen in flight as well as wheelchair assistance getting on and off the aircraft, Carole arranged for oxygen to be specially flown from Dallas to Sacramento that afternoon for the flight that evening. She then made special arrangements for someone with a wheelchair to meet us curbside at the airport, wheel him to the airplane, transfer him to an aisle wheelchair, help him into his seat, attach his oxygen tanks and hoses, check on him numerous times during the flight, transfer him back to a wheelchair, and have someone wheel him to curbside at the airport in Dallas. She even waited on the phone while I located his doctor to verify the amount of oxygen he would need. In other words, Carole spent as much time with us as was needed to totally alleviate what was an extremely stressful situation and allow us to turn our concern to my wife's father where it was needed. Carole's concern for our family in our time of need made us openly weep while on the phone with her.

We have never in all of our lives dealt with anyone with any company in any capacity who has exhibited such caring, compassion and true empathy for a customer as has Carole Goldstein. She placed the needs of a customer in very special circumstances above the need to make a profit for her company, which is very rare in this day and time. We are so grateful to Carole and American Airlines for the special treatment you provided us during our recent family crisis. Carole even contacted us the following Monday to make sure all went well with our flight and to ask how my wife's father was doing. We hope American Airlines realizes what a special treasure they have in Carole Goldstein. Rarely in one's lifetime does one have the opportunity to meet an individual so passionate in her concern for her fellow man. My grandmother spent her life as a nurse and a missionary in the Kentucky mountains, placing the health and well-being of others over her own. Not since my grandmother have I been fortunate enough to meet someone with those same special priorities as I have recognized in Carole Goldstein. If Carole performs these types of miracles on a regular basis, then we would like to nominate her for sainthood, because she has truly performed a miracle in helping us in our time of family crisis. Carole Goldstein is proof that angels really do exist.

Sincerely,
K. and K.C.
Dallas, Texas

He Wasn't Alone

I had been with American a little over a year and was flying as a first officer on a Super 80. I was at Chicago's O'Hare Airport and had gone to gate H-4 to sign in and check my messages.

An elderly gentleman came up to the desk, out of breath from running through the terminal. He asked for directions to our next Phoenix flight. He said he had just missed one flight due to weather and poor connections. I could see that he was upset, so I said something to calm him down like, "Not to worry, we have lots of service into Phoenix." As I was pulling up information on the computer, he suddenly collapsed on the other side of the counter.

I instantly ran to him, loudly calling for help. Two nearby passengers rushed to help. One was a doctor and the other a nurse. They immediately started CPR and the man started breathing again. I held his hand until the paramedics came and took him to the hospital. I then proceeded to my gate to fly my Atlanta flight. The flights were uneventful, and I couldn't stop thinking about our Phoenix passenger. When I returned to Chicago I was told the gentleman had passed away at the hospital.

I was able to get his name and address and shortly after, I wrote a letter to his family. I wanted them to know that he wasn't alone when he collapsed . . . I was with him. I held his hand, and he was at peace. I included my phone number in the letter.

About a week later I received a call from one of the man's daughters. She expressed her deepest appreciation on behalf of her family. She told me that my letter meant so much to them.

I remember losing my grandfather. He had attended my graduation from the Air Force Academy and was so proud. I was almost finished with my pilot training, and I desperately wanted him to see me get my wings.

I could easily relate to our Phoenix passenger's family and I knew if it were *my* dad or my grandfather I'd like to know someone was with him, that he wasn't alone.

Linda Green
Pilot
Dallas/Fort Worth

Customer Service — Beyond!

On March 12, 1998, a female customer was waiting for her luggage in the baggage claim area at Chicago's O'Hare airport.

As she watched, two men removed her bag from the carousel. She immediately advised an agent, who contacted Security. Mark McLaughlin, a supplies coordinator for American, overheard the call for help on the operations radio and went to the claim area to assist the agent.

At great personal risk, Mark held the men while waiting for the police. Mark McLaughlin saved a customer's bag from being stolen and allowed the Chicago police to make an arrest.

Donna Coyne
Managing Director, Customer Service
Chicago-O'Hare

Helping to Weather the Storm

September 1, 1992, was a day I wanted to be special. It was our 25th wedding anniversary and we had booked a vacation to the Bahamas. The trip became memorable, but for unhappy reasons—Hurricane Andrew hit the southeastern coast of the United States.

It wasn't easy after the storm, but AA was able to get us from Nassau to Miami. As we trudged through Miami terminal, I knew we weren't going anywhere soon; almost every square foot of floor had been staked out by stranded travelers.

When we reached the American ticket counter, true to form, there were blankets and pillows, hot coffee, pastries and—most important—words of encouragement.

During an ordeal that lasted for days, we witnessed the countless acts of kindness, charity and professionalism that I would soon come to recognize as the standard for American Airlines.

I realized then, as I do now, that our people really are a cut above the rest.

Karen Proffer
AAdvantage Reservations Agent
Cary, North Carolina

We'd Fly American Anytime

In 1996, American received a letter from an AA customer that complimented two flight attendants, Ms. Chris Novotny and Ms. Kathy Boyer.

The passenger's flight from San Jose to Chicago was delayed for four hours due to extreme weather in the Chicago area. Because of the delay, many passengers would miss their connecting flights and would be forced to stay overnight at the airport, because a large convention had taken all available hotel rooms in the Chicago area.

In addition to the tension of the storm and the resulting delay, en route the passengers received word of the tragic loss of TWA flight 800 to Paris that evening. Everyone was deeply upset.

The passenger was sitting next to a 14-year-old boy who was traveling alone and very concerned about missing his connecting flight to Boston. When they discovered that the boy had absolutely no money with him, the flight attendants used their personal credit card not only to phone the boy's mother and alleviate her fears, but to make overnight and future travel arrangements for him as well.

Both Chris and Kathy also rounded up all the available extra food on the airplane to give to those passengers who would now be stranded overnight in the airport.

Finally, as the passengers were leaving the plane, Kathy gave the boy $10 of her own money as an emergency precaution.

The passenger ended her letter with the comment that both she and her husband fly frequently for business and that they would be proud to fly American with Chris and Kathy anytime.

Patrick O'Keeffe
Managing Director, Flight Service
Headquarters

86

I Wouldn't Want It to Happen to Me!

A while ago, my husband and I were parked at the gate waiting for our flight from La Guardia to Chicago to back out. As I looked out the window, our first officer was walking around the plane doing his pre-flight check. Suddenly, a baggage cart drove by and a bag fell off the cart next to our plane.

The first officer spotted the bag, ran to it, and with hat in hand, picked up the bag and chased after the cart. Some observing maintenance workers joined in and stopped the cart so our first officer could catch up and reload the bag.

About half a dozen people looking out the windows started to clap, but as an employee I really felt proud of our first officer. Later, onboard, I had the opportunity to thank the first officer, and all he said was, "Hey, I wouldn't want it to happen to me!"

LaDonna Mathis
Flight Attendant
New York-La Guardia

Sometimes It's Okay to Bend the Rules

A few days before Christmas 1997, we got a call from an AAdvantage member. He had a terrible predicament. His wife was critically ill in a hospital in Oklahoma, and he wanted to use his AAdvantage miles to get his daughter home from Denmark, where she was a student.

American does not serve Denmark, so we arranged for his daughter to take a ferry to Copenhagen, then a British Airways flight to London. Since British Airways can't issue AAdvantage tickets, I asked if their personnel in Copenhagen would be willing to board a passenger without a ticket. Once the girl landed in London, I assured them, American would write the ticket and send it to British Airways.

A supervisor in Copenhagen agreed to this plan, and an AAdvantage supervisor authorized the paperwork.

With tremendous teamwork, resourceful thinking, and a willingness to bend normal procedures to fit the situation, American Airlines made the holiday song, "I'll Be Home for Christmas" a reality.

> Linda Jane Groth
> International AAdvantage Sales Representative
> Southern Reservations Office
> Fort Worth

You're Not Closing *My* Station

In early 1979, New Orleans was one of the expansion cities of the newly created deregulation era. The city opened with one daily flight and expanded to three shortly thereafter. Then, with the temporary grounding of the DC-10, New Orleans lost two flights. With just one flight, the station was on the brink of closure. George Riley, general manager for American in New Orleans, pleaded with Bob Baker, vice president of the Southern Division, to keep the station open and to convince Mr. Crandall not to close the city.

The city was given the opportunity and an ultimatum—to produce high load factors, high revenue, and outstanding performance.

At the time, there were six operations employees and one sales manager. These seven employees launched a vigorous campaign, working as a dedicated team, day-in and day-out, doing whatever it took to accomplish the directive and convince everyone of the great potential American had in the city of New Orleans.

The station eventually grew to a peak of 19 flights and a complement of over 100 employees. To this day, New Orleans contributes to the overall objectives of the company. I was proud to be one of the original seven employees that made American Airlines a household name in New Orleans.

Vito S. Cavaleri
Retired General Manager
New Orleans

Going the Extra Mile

Dear American,

I would like to commend Dallas/Fort Worth-based flight attendants Patti Wilson and Ronda Cates for service above and beyond the call of duty.

An hour into my flight from Long Beach to DFW, it dawned on me that I had forgotten to bring my 7-year-old son something back from Los Angeles as promised. I asked Ronda if there was anything onboard I could purchase. She told me there was nothing to buy, but she would see what she could come up with.

Fifteen minutes later, Ronda and Patti returned with a present they had beautifully put together—a gray AA travel mug filled with fruit, cookies and an activity booklet, on a white paper cloth decorated with a set of AA silver and blue wings.

Ronda and Patti didn't have to go to such trouble to bail me out. If they had told me there was nothing they could do I would have understood. Instead, they went the extra mile and never once made me feel I was inconveniencing them. What's more, they did it graciously and well.

Their random act of kindness put a smile on my face the rest of the way home, and made my son happy as well.

D.R.
Carrollton, Texas

Excerpts from *Flagship News*, March 23, 1997

We Have the Best People

Over a dozen years ago, as a new-hire in Reservations, I took a call from a very upset gentleman. We had aborted a takeoff out of O'Hare and, back in the terminal, the customer called to insist that we put him on another carrier. Although we had another flight leaving shortly, he didn't want to "risk" the lives of his wife or children on our plane. Sounding as professional as a proud new-hire can, I assured the gentleman we wouldn't take off again unless it was safe, and that our high standards for safety were why we didn't complete the initial takeoff. The man replied, "I don't believe you. You're only saying that because you work for American and they're paying you to say that." My response was quick and spontaneous, "No sir," I said. "It's the other way around. I could have gone to work for *any* airline, but *I chose* American because they have the highest standards for both safety and quality." After a brief pause, a much calmer gentleman thanked me and said he wanted to stay on AA.

Over the years, while my pride only grew deeper, the source of that pride changed. I came to realize American is not the best because of our high standards of safety and quality; and we're not the best because of our long list of industry firsts, such as our AAdvantage frequent flyer program. Nor are we the best because of our size, or the fact we have the most advanced technology in the industry. Quite simply, we are the best because we have the best *people*. And I count myself proud to be included in their number.

Michelle Britt
Reservations
Headquarters

Proud to Help Others

In 1964, while flying a DC-6 near Cincinnati, we were advised that a novice pilot in a small craft was in distress—lost, running low on fuel, and disoriented in thick cloud cover. We made contact with the terrified pilot, moved in as close as possible, and led him to safety. We received an FAA (Federal Aviation Administration) commendation for our actions.

Again on a stormy night, this time in 1984, while flying a Boeing 747 freighter to San Juan, we picked up a distress signal from a 32-foot sailboat on the edge of a tropical storm, 400 miles north of San Juan. We were able to coordinate the pertinent information with a U.S. Coast Guard search-and-rescue airplane which rescued the crew of the sailboat. I was very proud to have received a Coast Guard commendation for saving the lives of the five crew members onboard. I am equally proud that American Airlines has trained us so well to be able to help others in distress.

Bill Davenport
Captain and Former Chief Pilot
Washington

A Dedicated Friend

Dear American,

As an AAdvantage Platinum member, I travel frequently on business. After arriving in San Antonio recently, I discovered I had left my wallet at home. With only $4 in my pocket, I couldn't pick up my rental car or get to my appointment.

I explained the situation to Airport Operations Agent Nancy McMichael, who withdrew cash from her personal account at the ATM and loaned me enough money for a taxi and the parking charge at Dallas/Fort Worth. I don't know another airline whose employees would have helped in such a manner. I was a loyal customer before; now I'm a dedicated friend.

M.M.
Bedford, Texas

Excerpts from *Flagship News,* January 8, 1996

Stranded? Call American

A great airline is only as good as its employees. That's been driven home to me many times. But you never realize what exceptional people you're working with until you see the results firsthand.

Earlier this year, I was standing by for my flight from Dallas/Fort Worth, talking to Rosie, the agent working the flight.

As we talked, I found out that Rosie had recently discovered two stranded passengers, an elderly diabetic woman and her daughter, who were stranded for the evening in the airport. One had a full-fare ticket, the other a special pass. The women were trying to get to San Juan, and they were both very tired and upset.

Rosie insisted they come to her home where she gave them dinner, set up guest beds for them, and then brought them back to the airport in the morning for the first flight to San Juan. I feel so proud to be a part of a company that has such wonderful employees.

Mary Levin
Flight Attendant
New York-La Guardia

I Represent American Airlines

When I first joined American Airlines, I thought a flight attendant was someone whose basic job was to provide in-flight services to the traveling public. But over the years, interacting with thousands of passengers, I grew to learn that being an American employee means much more.

The travelers on my airplane knew that if something went wrong, I would save their lives. They knew I wasn't just an "employee" of some company, I was a representative of American Airlines. They could confide in me and rely on my opinion.

In 1968, immediately after the assassination of Robert Kennedy, Father Theodore Hesburgh, the renowned chancellor of the University of Notre Dame, traveled with me in First Class.

Prior to landing, he beckoned to me and asked if I would listen to the eulogy he was to give at Mr. Kennedy's memorial service. After listening to his well-chosen words spoken in his wonderfully comforting voice, I declared it "perfect." I felt so proud that he had the confidence to ask me to validate his eulogy, but when I really thought about it, I realized that he trusted me, a total stranger, because I was a representative of American Airlines.

Marti Seeds Schultz
Flight Attendant
Chicago-O'Hare, La Guardia

Great Service Is the Same in Every Language!

American Airlines flight attendants do everything they can to make passengers feel at home. Sometimes the results are even better than expected.

In the mid-1970s, a San Diego-New York flight was getting ready to depart. As our pre-boarding passengers were entering the plane, the agent brought on a small, elderly man in his 70s. We were informed that he was of Polish descent, spoke no English, and that his daughter would meet him in New York.

Fortunately, Audry, one of our flight attendants, was also Polish, and upon hearing about our elderly passenger, she launched into a conversation with the gentleman—in perfect Polish! The man's eyes gleamed, and he realized he was going to be in good hands for the entire flight. What he didn't realize—and neither did I—was that very soon, he would feel right at home.

As fate would have it, two other flight attendants also spoke Polish. Within minutes, three of the four flight attendants onboard began speaking in Polish. The odds of having three people that spoke Polish in the same crew are unbelievable. Our passenger must have thought he was in the "old country."

Now that's really putting the customers first.

Byron Morrill
Retired Captain
Los Angeles

The Fine Employees of American

Dear American,

Our flight from St. Maarten had a mechanical problem, and we were delayed several hours. The airport restaurant was closed, so we took a taxi to one nearby.

Unknown to us, the problem with the aircraft was fixed and the flight began boarding for an earlier-than-expected departure.

Near the end of our meal, a member of our party recognized Airport Operations Agent Sybouth Brown walking through the café searching for passengers. He told us about the change in plans and then hurried to his pickup truck, which carried six other passengers who had also left the airport. Mr. Brown radioed ahead to hold the plane and helped expedite us through Security.

Had it not been for Mr. Brown's willingness to search for missing passengers, we'd have missed our plane. We're glad that American has employees of such fine caliber.

D.M.
New York City

Excerpts from *Flagship News*, November 28, 1994

A Need for Speed

Mike Meyer, one of our crew chiefs, recalls that in the 1960s airlines competed intensely for the fastest airplane.

American designed a modification to the Convair 990, which broke a speed record. The modification included the addition of a tear-drop-shaped pod on the back end of the wing. It was so successful, that they applied the modification to the entire Convair 990 fleet.

This modification to the Convair 990 fleet kept people working in the hangar 24 hours a day, seven days a week. The men ate, slept, and virtually lived in the hangar. The wives of these men would bring a change of clothing to their husbands, and pass the clothing through the perimeter fence, so no one had to go home to change clothes.

This type of dedication is an integral part of what makes American Airlines successful.

Frederick J. Munkholm
Production Supervisor
Tulsa

Pitch In and Things Work Out Right

Back in the '50s, when CV-240s and DC-6s were flying between Chicago and New York, I was sent from Buffalo to Syracuse to replace a valve. When I finished, I checked with the agent to see what time the next flight to Buffalo was leaving so that I could return home. My wife and I had plans that night and she wanted me to be on time.

No flights were available any time soon to Buffalo, but there was a plane at the gate just about ready to leave for Niagara Falls, which would put me on my way home. The flight would stop in Rochester. When we landed in Rochester, the first officer came back to my seat and said, "I've discovered a hydraulic leak in the belly around the rear access door. Would you check it out?"

I knew everyone on that flight was as eager to get home as I was, so I hoped I could help. As fate would have it, it turned out that the leak was coming from a valve in the same area as the Convair I had just repaired. I had extra parts with me that I had been carrying for the plane I serviced in Syracuse, and was able almost immediately to fix the valve.

The agent working the flight in Rochester picked up some hydraulic fluid from United Airlines and topped off the tank. With everyone pitching in, our departure was only a little late.

When we arrived in Niagara Falls, the personnel director from Buffalo, Don Davis, was at the bottom of the stairs. He said, "We were wondering where the mechanic came from to repair this airplane." He sure was surprised to see me—and gave me a ride back to Buffalo! I guess that's just the American way. When everyone pitches in, things work out right. And my wife was especially happy because I made it home on time!

Ransom D. Converse
Retired Senior Mechanic, A&E/A&P
Los Angeles

A Great Job

To: Gloria Ann Ford
Domestic Sales Dept./Western Reservations Office

From: D.A. DiCarlo—Southern Reservations Office

Re: Customer Phone Call of October 18, 1989

I have not been with the company long but I must say that this is absolutely the best agent compliment I have ever received.

A gentleman called to make emergency travel arrangements after learning that his daughter had slipped into a coma and was not expected to live through the night. Although he was not able to go right away, he set up reservations for his wife and other daughter to fly to Cleveland. He said his first American Airlines contact was Ms. Ford and that she was just beautiful. Ms. Ford offered every option available. She went out of her way to make sure that his family's needs were met and that everything was within his price range. When his family boarded their flight, they were treated like royalty. They felt like all the crew knew about their situation and made sure that his family was comfortable throughout their flight. When his family arrived, his daughter was still in a coma, but as soon as his wife went into her room, she regained consciousness and smiled at her mother. Within the day, the father received a phone call from his daughter who, earlier, was not even supposed to live. After staying a while in

Cleveland, the family finally had to come back—the return flight was no different from the departure. He says he now knows why American Airlines is the world's best, and that American Airlines is now his family's airline.

The father extended his gratitude to the whole airline for our support to his family, and a special thanks to you, Ms. Ford, for making him feel like his needs were special to American. Ms. Ford you did a great job.

Thank You.

I Can Make the World a Little Brighter

My motto is, "The way to make the world better is to make someone else's world a little better each day."

In some ways, the world of a telephone reservations agent is small, in others, it can be huge. I may not fly the planes, or supervise a crew—and I don't deliver small children to their smiling grandparents for summer vacation, but with my voice, I can reach an unlimited world, touching passengers over the phone each day. With each call I take, I want the passenger to hear a smile in *my* voice. But more than that, I want to feel like I've put a smile on the face of each passenger I talk with during the call.

When I talk with an elderly person planning a trip, I take a minute to listen to their plans and take an interest in where they're going. Sometimes I'll ask how many grandchildren they have or if the trip is for a special occasion, like a birthday or anniversary. It only takes a minute, and I've heard some pretty interesting stories over the years. There's nothing more rewarding than the heart felt "thank you" of a business traveler when I've just booked him on the last seat on the last flight home that day, so he can see his kids (for the first time in weeks) before they go to bed. Sometimes I'll joke with a mother of small children, harried by all the commotion going on while she's trying to make reservations. I like our passengers to know they've got someone on their side.

As reservations agents, we may be grounded, but I like to feel I'm just getting our passengers in the right mood so our flight crews will have an easier job. We're doing our part to make a person want to call American again. I believe there is more to my job than just doing it well. Just for a moment, while I've got that passenger on the phone, I can make the world a little brighter or their day a little easier. Sometimes I feel like "Dear Abby," but small moments add up, and when I'm making passengers smile, my day is a little brighter, too.

Helen E. Wilson
Reservations Agent
Tucson

We Do What Needs to Be Done

On February 1, 1997, 200 passengers were scheduled to depart on Flight #46 from Chicago to London.

Boarding had started at 8 p.m., and at 8:30 p.m. Maintenance told Customer Service that there was a problem with the main landing gear that would cause a lengthy delay.

Patrick Winkler was the international departure coordinator and Hans Kuehn was working as the number one agent. Hans immediately notified our passengers of the delay and Patrick prepared for the worst. He knew that if the equipment went out of service, he'd need meals and hotel accommodations for 200 passengers.

At 10 p.m., Maintenance pulled the aircraft. Since Patrick had already made all of the necessary arrangements, the process of relocating our passengers to hotels went quite smoothly. Hans stayed with our customers that needed special help or needed to make phone calls to London. By midnight, everyone was tucked in.

The only available replacement for Flight #46's equipment was a smaller plane. Both Patrick and Hans stayed to wait for the new aircraft, and to make arrangements for 25 passengers who would now have to be booked on alternate flights to London.

Rather than turn this flight over to the morning shift, both Patrick and Hans elected to stay the course. Special arrangements had to be made with Ramp Service to X-ray all luggage so it could be transferred to the new equipment. New itineraries for all customers connecting in

London had to be developed and printed out for each passenger affected.

By 9 in the morning, they had completed all the arrangements required and started working with the customers as they returned to the airport from the hotel. Both men had been working for almost 20 hours. Our customers were so pleased to see Patrick and Hans the next morning, and to know that every detail had been handled for them.

Donna Coyne
Managing Director, Customer Service
Chicago-O'Hare

Some Agents Sell Tickets—Others Build a Business

Can you imagine customers willingly waiting in line for a specific ticket agent?

That's the situation in Southfield, Michigan, where it's been my pleasure to work with Terry McCracken.

Terry exemplifies the American Airlines spirit—a combination of professionalism, good humor, efficiency and knowledge.

We worked for nine years together in our Southfield ticket office, and every day I would watch repeat customers come in, get in Terry's line and wait for her to help them.

To me, Terry exemplifies what American Airlines is all about.

Diana E. Miklos
Admirals Club Service Representative
Detroit

Who's Flying the Plane?

I spent the last few years of my career flying the MD-11 to Europe. During my crew rest time I used to like to circulate through the cabin talking to the passengers. One of my favorite questions was, "Who's flying the plane?" Although some asked in jest, I could sense relief from others as I talked about computers, the crew's competence and, of course, "George"—our name for autopilot. Another frequently asked question was, "What are the things at the ends of the wings?" I would smile and give my standard answer: "They're winglets. And they're bent up like that because the airplane was too big to fit through the doors at the factory." After a few laughs, I'd tell them the real reason and take on the next question. Sometimes they weren't always questions—they were comments. The one I heard most often sums up what I think makes us great. They'd say, "The difference between American and other airlines is that the American crews are so professional. They're interested in their passengers and genuinely care." After spending my entire career with American, I would have to say, this comment is true.

Ernest C. Johnson
Retired Captain
Chicago-O'Hare

Expect the Unexpected

As American Airlines fleet service clerks, we're trained to be ready for everything, including the last-minute and unexpected.

A small station like El Paso doesn't usually handle planes as large as a 757. One quiet September night, with a small crew on duty, we were notified by airport security that a 757 was being diverted our way for a medical emergency. The plane was just minutes away. With only six men and one crew chief, we quickly moved aircraft and made way for the "big bird." Fortunately, we got everything in place in time for a safe landing. The local paramedics were able to remove our passenger for the necessary treatment, and we were able to get the 757 back out and on its way with a minimum delay. It was quite a night (or morning— 2:30 a.m.)! I was proud to be a part of a winning team. Thank you Sammy Hernandez, George Seelig, Danny Legarreta, Steve Czaster, Joe Kall, Louie Ramo and Felix Casas. I was really proud of the job you guys did that night.

Alexander Alba
Fleet Service Clerk
El Paso

Take It Step By Step

My mother always told me that while the end result is important, it's each little step from start to finish that really matters.

Not long ago, a young lady arrived at our ticket counter in Antigua to check-in for a flight to San Juan. She presented her ticket, and when asked for her passport, she discovered it missing. She looked through her pockets and purse but it wasn't there. She told the agent that she obviously lost her passport. Our agent then advised her that because she was traveling on an international flight, she must produce a valid passport, or she couldn't leave the island. The lady instantly broke into tears. In fact, she got quite hysterical. Our agent immediately left his position and escorted the lady to an area away from the other passengers so she could calm down.

The agent asked the lady a few questions and found out where she had stayed and contacted the hotel, which in turn was actually able to locate the taxi that brought her to the airport. Step-by-step the agent retraced her movements—but her passport was still nowhere to be found. The next step was to locate her luggage and check each bag. By this time the agent was trying to think how he was going to tell her she wasn't leaving Antigua today.

Upon searching the luggage, the passport was found. It was packed neatly between a pair of blue jeans. As the passenger removed it the agent exhaled, "Thank God, because I didn't want to tell you that you couldn't depart." The young lady asked, "How did you stay so calm knowing that?" He smiled and said, "It's part of my job."

I think the important lesson is that the agent could have given up along the way, but he didn't. He went step-by-step and finally solved the problem.

C.F. Roberts
Passenger Service Agent
Antigua

We Can Fix Anything

Every once in a while something goes wrong for one of our passengers. The best thing about American Airlines is that we have the systems in place to fix almost any problem.

We had a passenger at our Guadalajara, Mexico, station who had lost his ticket. Because it was a Saturday and his travel agent in Denver was closed, we couldn't simply get the necessary fare and other information we needed.

We asked the customer to call his wife at home to obtain his ticket number from her copy of his itinerary. We then called our AAdvantage team in Mexico City with the ticket number and they were able to provide all the missing data. We quickly reissued our passenger's ticket. I was very proud that teamwork allowed us to help this passenger.

Laura D. Martinez
Reservations/City Ticket Office Agent
Guadalajara JAL, Mexico

There's a Lot I Can Teach You!

I joined American Airlines in 1988, and shortly thereafter, met Mr. Crandall at a planning conference in Dallas.

He asked me how long I had been with the company, and I told him I was a new employee. He then asked me about my background, and I explained that I had just joined American from the cargo airline, Flying Tigers, where I had previously spent 11 years. Before that, I had spent another 10 years at various aircraft manufacturing companies.

I'll never forget his comment to me: "Welcome aboard, we have a lot to learn from you." I went home that night feeling very good about my new company, and I feel just as good 10 years later.

Alan R. Glad
Senior Technical Representative
Component Maintenance
Tulsa

Think Quickly

One of the best things about American Airlines is that everyone is encouraged to think on their feet. They don't hire you just for your job function, but for your resourcefulness. It certainly makes things interesting.

One episode comes to mind: I was between flights, checking passenger loads for my next trip, when an elderly woman anxiously approached the security guard standing next to me. She was speaking in a language neither of us understood, but she was obviously upset. Somehow, I was able to communicate to her that I needed to see her ticket. Her ticket told me that she had just arrived from Korea, via Los Angeles. So I called Korean Airlines and asked for a Korean-speaking agent to translate for me.

I soon discovered that this woman did not speak a word of English, was lost, unable to locate her checked luggage, and couldn't find her family who was supposed to meet her. Since I had at least two hours before my next flight, I offered to help. With her carry-ons in hand, I escorted her to the baggage claim area for the Los Angeles flight. We located her luggage, and it was only a matter of moments before her family anxiously ran through the doors, obviously relieved to see that she had arrived safely and was in good hands.

As I stood in my uniform by this woman, I was proud to think that her relatives would remember American Airlines as the company that took good care of their family—and would surely do the same in the future.

When I returned to the gate, I told the security guard that the woman was reunited with her family and that everything had worked out just fine. He just looked at me and asked, "How did you ever think to call Korean Airlines to translate?" It was then that I realized what my job at American was really all about.

Andrew Wright
Purser
Miami

Part of the Job

It was a rainy evening, about 7 p.m., and as I was leaving the airport terminal to go home, I saw an older woman standing by the baggage carousel obviously confused.

She spotted my uniform and spoke to me in Spanish, my native language, and asked me to help her.

She had arrived in San Francisco on another airline three hours late. Her daughter was to have met her, but could not be found. I took her to the competitor's ticket counter and received no help. We went to the arrival gate—no daughter—and again, no help from the staff. I was embarrassed for them. I asked to speak to a supervisor. We waited 20 minutes, and after the supervisor didn't show up, I decided to take the passenger back to American Airlines and find her daughter.

We called and reached her at home. She was surprised her mom was at the airport, because the other carrier had told her she wasn't on the flight and would be arriving tomorrow.

She came right out to the airport and had a wonderful reunion with her mom, whom she hadn't seen in three years.

I gave them my number in the event they had any other problems. Two days later, the daughter called me to say they had cancelled the return trip on our competitor and booked American.

I had spent almost four hours helping this woman, and I know I would do the exact same thing again if the situation presented itself. I consider it part of my job.

Renato Monteverde
Customer Service Agent
American Eagle
San Francisco

A Helping Hand

"Pops" is an American mechanic in St. Martin. Following the last hurricane that devastated the island, Pops recounted that an American 757 was sent to the island loaded with relief supplies along with an American Airlines construction crew. Their mission: re-build the houses of all the American employees on St. Martin!

Pops said, "These guys would not quit! I started them off with coffee at 7 a.m. and had to make them come down off the roof for a beer at 6 p.m.!"

After repairing the homes of all American Airlines employees, the crew donated thousands of pounds of additional construction and relief supplies to the other residents of the island.

Captain Mark Hettermann
Winds of Washington Newsletter, December 1995

Sometimes You Need Great Passengers to Make a Great Airline

In July 1990, I was a flight attendant on flight #400 from Miami to San Juan. While in flight, our navigational computer failed and we diverted to Nassau for an emergency landing.

Our captain, Mike Carroll, solved the problem without the need of an A300 mechanic. Now we only needed Maintenance to inspect the system and sign off on the paperwork. Things were looking good.

Then we learned we needed additional fuel to continue to San Juan or we'd have to return to Miami. Since we didn't have an account with the fuel supplier in Nassau, we'd have to pay cash. Several of our First Class passengers overheard the conversation between our captain and ground personnel and decided that rather than return to Miami, they would raise the cash amongst themselves to purchase the fuel. The total was thousands of dollars.

Miami-based lead agent Pilar Carro took charge and recorded the names of those passengers who volunteered, so they could be reimbursed upon arrival in San Juan.

The rest of the flight went well, and all of our passengers were very appreciative of those First Class passengers who made it possible for us to continue.

We have a wonderful airline, but we also carry wonderful passengers.

Doug Martinez
Flight Attendant
Washington

A Great Honor

I was so proud when in 1966 the National Aeronautics and Space Administration (NASA) wrote Mr. C.R. Smith to thank me for the continued and exceptional service that I provided representatives of NASA's manned spacecraft center in Houston and the Grumman aircraft unit developing the lunar module.

To have directly or even indirectly contributed to our nation's efforts to carry our astronauts to the moon was a great honor.

Richard Warburton
Retired Sales Representative
New York

Never Say Never

Sometimes, all you need to turn "can't do" into "can do," is a little creativity.

In 1977, I was to fly a DC-10 from New York to Los Angeles a couple of days before Christmas. There was a very heavy headwind, and dispatch wanted to off-load some passengers so that we could add additional fuel. But it was December 23, and we knew our passengers probably wouldn't be able to get another flight out until after Christmas Day. So, we revisited our flight plan and re-checked the conditions.

I noticed that the heavy winds abated below 20,000 feet. Our plan was filed to fly at 35,000 feet. We decided to file a new flight plan, and left New York with 20,000 feet as our cruise altitude. We kept all of our passengers onboard and added Phoenix as a fuel stop if necessary. Eventually, we went up to 22,000 feet. By the time we got to the Rocky Mountains, the winds had lessened, and I was able to ascend to our original 35,000 feet.

Bottom line: we arrived in Los Angeles 20 minutes *early*, didn't have to refuel, and got everybody home for the holidays.

Bud Vietor
Retired Captain
Los Angeles

120

There Are Lots of Ways to Give Extra Care

One day we were loading freight and one of the guys came upon a beautiful model of a sailing ship in a really flimsy crate. We were on a time deadline. No time to try to re-crate the art, but all of us were concerned that it might get broken. The best we could do was to place a big note on the crate that said:

"I'm just a sailing ship far from the sea, and if you would take the time to look you will see, I'm as fragile as can be. So won't you please take extra care of me?"

A few weeks later we received a nice letter from the consignee. His ship arrived unscathed.

Edward L. Churnetski
Retired Airport Operations Agent
Air Freight
Newark

Employees Are Family

How you treat your own is often a clue as to how you treat others.

In the case of American Airlines, I never have a doubt that the customers are getting the very best care. I've experienced it first-hand over a span of three decades.

In the 1970s, when I was about to give birth, my mother rushed from the East Coast to be by my side. The special captain who kept her informed of my progress, and the special flight attendant who drove my mother 30 miles to the hospital to make sure she would be there in time, were indicative of a caring crew.

In the 1980s, when my parents died and I had to return to the East Coast, it was a special American Airlines crew who consoled me and my son along the way.

In the 1990s, when an earthquake devastated my town of Northridge, California, it was a group of very special flight attendants who provided my family and others in the area with food and water.

With this kind of compassion for each other, you know our customers are getting the best of service.

Harriet B. Johnson
Flight Attendant
Los Angeles

"It's part of my job . . ."

It had been a long night and I was really tired at the end of my shift. I could hardly wait to board the TrAAm to the employee parking lot and go home. Relaxing into my seat, I noticed an unattended bag in the seat next to me.

Unable to locate the owner onboard the TrAAm, I got off at the next stop, and using our reservations system, identified the passenger's destination from the name tag on the bag. The flight was leaving in 10 minutes, and the plane was 14 gates away! I ran down the ramp to the departure gate and pulled the agent aside.

Just as I was explaining about the bag, a worried-looking woman approached and began frantically asking questions in Spanish. She spoke no English, and as the agent tried to answer her, the lady suddenly noticed the bag I was holding. Her face brightened as she pointed to the bag, "Gracías, muchas gracías!" She grabbed the bag and ran toward the boarding gate to catch her flight. At the door she turned and smiled at me. I smiled back. It made me feel very good to help a stranger—but that's my job.

So ends another shift at American Airlines.

Tim Keyrouze
Fleet Service Clerk
Dallas/Fort Worth

It's All About Instinct

We found a story in the August 1995 issue of *Winds of Washington* that we think is typical of the American spirit.

That March day in Jacksonville, Florida started early in the afternoon for Captain Joel Miller and First Officer Joel Benson. They were scheduled to fly to Dallas and then onto San Antonio, Texas. Thunderstorms were in the forecast for Texas, but it looked like they would be lucky today, as the line had moved east of Dallas with no problems at the airport.

Their flight to Dallas was indeed routine. They then took off for San Antonio with no significant weather predicted. Winds in the area were reported mild at 10 knots. As they were on final approach to San Antonio Airport's runway 30, both pilots noticed a new picture on their radar screen . . . significantly changed from a mere three minutes earlier. In a horseshoe pattern, running west to north, strong weather or cell activity was sprouting as they watched!

Captain Miller continued his approach. As he passed 2,500 feet, San Antonio tower reported no significant change in its winds. At 1,500 feet, the field was fully in sight with no sign of precipitation. However, with his deteriorating radar picture and pure instinct, Captain Miller decided to abandon his approach.

Captain Miller's instinctive decision was fortuitous. As his throttles were advanced to "go-around" thrust, they were hit with wind shear. Airspeed almost stopped. They lost altitude. Severe turbulence followed. Captain Miller, knowing his escape route, turned to 110° and airspeed and altitude slowly increased. However, the turn was interrupted several times as severe air turbulence came in waves and caused both airspeed and altitude to stagnate.

Captain Miller and First Officer Benson continued to climb until they found clear air. Meanwhile, in the cabin, one of the flight attendants described the experience: "It felt like we hit a wall. The nose went up. It was like a big hand had grabbed the plane and was shaking us. Our passengers were terrified."

After turning north toward their Austin alternate, a quick look at the on-board radar showed the developing line of thunderstorms they had just escaped working its way through central Texas. Austin had the potential to rerun what they had just encountered. Dallas was reporting thunderstorms in the area. Dispatch said Austin or Dallas . . . Captain Miller said Houston! They landed in Houston at 1:19 a.m. without difficulty. Dispatch advised refueling and a "go" to San Antonio, with an added, "Oh, by the way, additional storms were forming 40 miles west, moving east!"

Captain Miller decided his passengers and crew had seen enough for one evening. They elected to stay in Houston.

It was now 3:00 a.m., and with only one night agent on duty, Captain Miller, First Officer Benson and four crew members (Mary Arthur O'Sullivan, Mia McLeod, Linda Smith and William Swartz), ended flight #1063.

In a deserted terminal, the Washington-based crew

booked every passenger into hotel rooms and made arrangements for their continued passage the following day. They ended their long day at 4:00 a.m.

This crew was tested repeatedly, both externally by the weather, and by internal pressures to get the passengers to their proper destination. Through it all, Captain Miller remained a captain in the best tradition of all who had come before him. His first officer assisted him flawlessly. He acted in the best interest of his passengers and he instinctively made the right decisions.

Captain Mark Hettermann
Winds of Washington Newsletter, August 1995

Trust

One day, when I was working the receiving dock at La Guardia, I saw a lady was trying to ship some food to her family in Haiti. She soon discovered that she didn't have enough money to pay for the shipping. We could all tell that she felt very bad, and I thought she was about to cry. So I went into the office and spoke to the agent, Connie Covington. Between us, we decided to help her. We went through our pockets and came up with enough money to get her shipment on its way. She was very grateful, and thanked us repeatedly. She insisted she would get the money back to us right away. And just a few days later, she did return to repay us.

Frank Magazino
Retired Clerk
New York-LaGuardia

A Little Ingenuity Goes a Long Way

One busy night at Kennedy many years ago, we had a full plane, ready to pull away from the gate. Just as we got the departure salute from the agent on the ground, I heard a frantic voice calling, "Wait!" A flight attendant rushed into the cockpit to tell me that one of our passengers had suddenly realized that he had all the keys to the house, car, garage, etc., on the plane with him, while his wife, unknowingly, was on the ground seeing him off. We devised a quick plan and sent the flight attendant back to the passenger (who by then was just on the other side of the cockpit door) to retrieve the keys. We packed up the keys with a short message concerning to whom the keys were to be delivered, then placed them in a flight engineer's glove to be dropped out the window to our push crew.

The delay amounted to no more than a couple of minutes. We learned later that all went well; the keys were delivered to the passenger's wife, and the flight engineer's glove was returned! A little ingenuity, driven by a desire to solve a passenger's problem, is all it took.

H.G. Robinson
Retired Captain
New York-Kennedy

In Good Hands

Several years ago, a major airline strike grounded most of the transcontinental carriers. American was the only one still flying. Needless to say, our Los Angeles terminal was jammed with people trying to get flights. Some were involved in family emergencies.

When I came to work early one morning, I saw a young Japanese girl standing near the information counter looking absolutely terrified. When I tried to speak to her, she just stood there without acknowledging me—frozen, with big tears in her eyes. Our information agent told me that she had tried to help the young lady, but couldn't get any response.

Our passenger service manager's office was nearby, so I took her by the hand and brought her to the office. She had two envelopes with her. One contained a TWA receipt from Tokyo to Los Angeles along with a valid flight coupon from Los Angeles to Washington, D.C. The other envelope contained a letter from her husband, who was an American stationed at an army base near Washington.

Clearly, with TWA on strike, and this young lady reluctant to communicate, she wasn't going anywhere. My first task was to somehow find her a seat on one of our Washington flights. I contacted our reservations manager and asked him to try to find one seat.

American's systems work. Somehow our people cleared a seat on the 11 p.m. flight that night.

My next job was to try to find her husband at the army base, explain the situation, and advise him of her new flight plans. When I finally tracked him down, he was greatly relieved that she was safe and in good hands. He promised he would be there to meet her flight.

As I was speaking, the young lady recognized I was speaking to her husband and her face lit up. I gave her the phone, and they conversed for a moment; she was so relieved.

We left the office and I asked our Admirals Club skipper to take charge of her well-being, get her some lunch, and make sure she boarded her flight without incident.

I said goodbye to a totally different young lady—this one was smiling and at ease. I couldn't help but think that the power of compassion is an amazing thing.

Bud Saunders
Retired Special Representative
Los Angeles Sales

Doing the Job the Right Way

Recently, during weather delays at Dallas/Fort Worth, we had passengers requiring assistance on every flight. I was the only one on duty after 10 p.m. Our last flight, which usually arrived at 11:20 p.m., came in at 3:30 a.m.!

A family arrived at the gate area around 8 p.m. to wait for the last flight. They were elderly people and had driven 40 miles to the airport. Throughout the evening, as I was meeting my other flights, I talked with them, just passing the time. They were very nice, sweet people. Since all the shops and restaurants had closed around midnight, I went to our break room, made fresh coffee, and took it upstairs and served them. I sat with them until they finished their coffee. I was surprised that my little gesture made them so happy. One of the ladies, who explained that her brother-in-law is a pilot with another airline, said this was customer service "above and beyond the call of duty." She was so appreciative, she took my name, and said, "I think this is how American makes the difference." To me, I was only helping them, and doing my job the *right* way.

Banu Hurt
Gate Agent
San Antonio

131

Customers Expect Initiative

Flight procedures at small airports with limited operating hours sometimes call for creativity and flexibility. American Eagle Captain J.F. Ruiz and First Officer R.A. Contreras, showed all of this and more on a departure from Dominica.

The airport in Dominica operates only from sunrise to sunset. It was close to sunset when Captain Ruiz landed his American Eagle to pick up a full load of passengers.

Everything was shutting down. There were no communications, no flight instructions, no nothing. Captain Ruiz told his 64 passengers that he'd be right back. He and his first officer took off with an empty plane to gain enough altitude so that he could radio a dispatcher at another center. Once he had achieved enough altitude for a strong signal, he radioed the station at the nearby island of Point-à-Pitre to obtain a flight release and important fuel requirements. After successfully obtaining all of the required authorizations, he then returned to Dominica, picked up his passengers, and left with only a small delay.

If Captain Ruiz hadn't acted with such initiative, our passengers would have had to spend another night in Dominica at great expense and inconvenience. I was the dispatcher for that flight, and it made me proud to be an American employee.

Grace Hunt
Flight Dispatcher
Dallas/Fort Worth

The Birth of Air Navigation

In 1996, I had the privilege of visiting with retiree Warren J. Weldon. Warren started with American in 1935, when he was 19 years old, at Meacham Field in Fort Worth, Texas. He was originally hired to maintain our aircraft and ground radios.

In 1935, air navigation was in its infancy, and the method as told by Warren was:

> We had nothing but a 4-tower low frequency radio station near the airport for air navigation. When the ceiling was low or there was fog, the flight superintendent at Fort Worth went up to the roof of the hangar. He would listen to the sound of the approaching aircraft outside and then he would call downstairs to our radio operator who would then tell the pilot where he was in relation to the airport.

American decided to upgrade its navigation systems and leased equipment from the Lorenz Company in Germany and first tested it at Meacham Field. Warren Weldon installed the first experimental airline instrument landing system (ILS) in America, and after it was found to be successful, the U.S. Government put it in nationwide.

Warren Weldon was, for me, one of our most pioneering employees, who not only contributed so much to American Airlines, but to the entire aviation industry.

In 1946, the year our maintenance base opened, he moved to Tulsa to become foreman of the radio shop. He continued his career until he retired in 1978.

Warren passed away in 1997, but I will never forget the twinkle in his eye and the pride he displayed when we spoke about his company.

Kay Webb
Special Projects Administrator
Maintenance & Engineering Center
Tulsa

There Are Pilots, and There Are Pilots!

During a recent trip, a flight attendant asked one of our first officers, Lloyd Bertsfield, to perform a task above and beyond his duties.

A First Class passenger had accidentally dropped a $16,000 bracelet in the forward toilet and was hysterical.

First Officer Bertsfield put on the rubber gloves from one of the emergency kits and was able to reach in and retrieve the bracelet.

There are pilots and there are pilots. Lloyd Bertsfield is a very special pilot. I'd fly with anyone this conscientious anytime.

Rod Carson
Captain
San Francisco

We're Never Really off Duty

On a recent trip to Kansas City, a returning passenger was rushing to give a speech at the International Customer Service Association Conference. As he attempted to exit the parking garage, he realized he only had a company check, and the garage attendant refused to accept it.

I was working as a passenger service agent in Kansas City, was off duty and returning home, when I noticed the gentleman's dilemma.

As he was preparing to head up to the terminal to get some cash, I asked him if he needed any help. He explained his problem and I immediately gave him $20 along with my business card.

The gentleman made his meeting on time, returned the $20, and in a thank-you note to Mr. Crandall, mentioned that he used my example of outstanding customer service as part of his speech!

Stanley L. Busken
Passenger Service Agent
Kansas City

We Prove We're Good Everyday

Sometimes, no matter how good you are, you have to prove yourself over and over again. At American Airlines, we do this willingly.

Recently, American Airlines entered into a multi-faceted business relationship with Canadian Airlines. When Canadian Airlines moved their accounting functions to our facility in Tulsa, we were truly put to the test. Many Canadian customers felt that their airline was disloyal for moving part of its operation out of Canada. So, every day, our department had to prove itself on everything we worked on.

In the true AA spirit we banded together as a team and worked days and nights, as well as some weekends, to convince our new Canadian partners and their customers that we could do our jobs well. We also found that even our customers really liked our service. Their receivables never looked so good!

Mr. Capozzi, I know you will probably want to publish stories about our amazing flight crews or our dedicated airport agents, but I think it is important for people to know that the American Airline spirit is alive and well, on the front lines all the way through to an accounting department in Tulsa.

Theresa Farinas
Account Specialist
Tulsa

Watch What You Say

I've learned to always watch what I say because sometimes you don't know who you're talking to.

On one occasion, our crew was standing on a jetbridge waiting to board our outbound flight. The inbound passengers were almost all off the plane. A connecting passenger requiring assistance was helped into a wheelchair next to the aircraft door, but there was no agent available to push the woman to her connecting flight.

Seeing this situation, our captain greeted her, and *he* pushed her up the jetbridge to the gate agent. As a flight attendant, I've done this a few times, but I've never seen one of our captains help a passenger this much.

Later, after we had gotten off the ground and things had calmed down, I remarked to our first flight attendant that I thought our captain was a very special person. She said, "I know; I'm married to him!"

Jerry Hare
Flight Attendant
Dallas/Fort Worth

Exceptional Service
Doesn't Need Management's Approval

A neighbor of mine was called up for active duty during the Gulf War in 1991. Unfortunately, he suffered a heart attack in Saudi Arabia a few weeks later, and was airlifted to a military hospital in Germany.

His wife, Barbara, booked reservations in the Main Cabin from Tulsa to O'Hare to Frankfurt to join John. Knowing she would be traveling alone, I figured the least I could do was see her off to Chicago. I found her sitting in the departure lounge all alone, waiting to board the aircraft. I accompanied her to the ticket lift area, where I told Shirley, the ticket lift agent, about Barbara and John's plight. That's all I had to do.

Shirley looked at Barbara's ticket and said, "We can do better than that; First Class still has seats available," and upgraded her. She also told Barbara that she would be met by an agent at O'Hare.

On each leg of her trip to Europe, Barbara was met by American agents who handled her needs, and flight crews who took extra time to talk to her about a variety of topics to relax her. Her ticket to Europe was upgraded to Business Class. Barbara was amazed by the VIP treatment she was receiving. When she arrived in Frankfurt, an American Airlines representative helped her through Customs.

John was recovering at an acceptable rate, and much of their conversation was about the extra effort AA personnel had made for her.

Today, John is in excellent health and practicing medicine in Tulsa. He and Barbara are two of American's best "sales people" in town.

The bottom line: the American "Spirit of Greatness" was demonstrated in the kind of VIP treatment that was provided by front-line employees. Management has empowered employees to do the right thing, and there is no need for higher management to get involved because the employees who "operate" the airline know that they are capable of making the right decisions.

Karl J. Knight
Retired Manager
Station and Eagle Surveillance
Tulsa

Taking Action

April 2, 1996

American Airlines, Inc.
Consumer Relations

Dear American,

Re: Flight #888, Oklahoma City to Chicago,
    March 17, 1996

I was taking my wife to the Mayo Clinic in Rochester, MN and, about 5 minutes out of Chicago-O'Hare airport, one of the flight attendants began to read off the connecting flights. We did not hear a connecting flight given to Rochester, MN, but did to Rochester, NY.

You guessed it! Our local travel agent had booked us to Rochester, N.Y. I immediately notified one of the flight attendants and they took action. When we landed, the previously requested wheelchair was there for my wife. The American ticket agent, at the gate flight #888 pulled up to, was at the cargo door, had pulled our three pieces of luggage off, and had them sitting beside us within three minutes after we had exited your aircraft.

Now the "really" good part. Jacqui Christian, one of the flight attendants, personally took us "in tow." She parked Sherry, my wife, and the wheelchair attendant, in a waiting area, and then walked me a quarter of a mile to the American ticket desk, where we were quickly rebooked to Rochester, MN. Then Jacqui walked me back to where we had left my wife.

Jacqui was so willing to go the "extra mile" that I wanted you to know what a wonderful feeling it gave us to have her guidance, especially since it was our first time at Chicago-O'Hare.

And yes, Jacqui, my lovely wife is doing better, thanks to you, the Mayo Clinic and the service of American Airlines.

Best Wishes,
D.H.
Altus, Oklahoma

It's My Job

Ms. Donna Darrow, an Admirals Club manager, recently wrote a commendation letter about Steven Emmert, the First Class flight attendant on a Miami-Chicago trip. In her letter, Ms. Darrow mentioned that in addition to his extremely dedicated and professional service, Emmert used each passenger's name throughout the entire trip. When she asked him how he could possibly remember everyone's name he simply responded, "It's my job!"

Editor

FROM THE HEART

Get Involved — It Means a Lot

A few years ago, while based in Los Angeles, I was working a flight from Dallas/Fort Worth to Burbank. While setting up the back galley of a Super 80, a passenger boarded, took a seat, and began to cry. Concerned, I said, "If you'd like to talk, I'd like to listen." She told me her little brother, who was then in his late 30s, was suffering from AIDS and expected to die soon. As we talked, her feelings of guilt became clear—they had not spoken in 15 years. Her brother's nurse had found her telephone number in his address book and had contacted her. Her brother was unaware that his big sister was on her way to comfort him.

When the plane landed in Burbank, I offered to give the woman, unfamiliar with California and overcome with emotion, a ride to her brother's home. As we drove through

North Hollywood, she talked about how close they had been while growing up and laughed about the crazy things they'd done together so many years ago.

As we pulled up to his home, she thanked me, turned to leave my car and froze. Terrified, she asked me to come into the house with her. Concerned for her brother's privacy, I declined. She persisted and I finally agreed. The nurse took us into her brother's bedroom. When he saw his sister, his frail face lit up like a Christmas tree. After a few moments of getting acquainted and celebrating this brother-sister reunion, I gave my telephone number to the woman and left. A few weeks later she called to let me know that her brother had passed away quietly, happy and with dignity.

Looking back, I am proud that I took the time to get involved. I thank God that I was able to assist in reuniting a family and to meet such wonderful people. I hope those who read this story will be inspired to treat all sick people with the respect, compassion and dignity that they deserve.

Shannon Veedock
Flight Attendant
Washington-Reagan National

Back on Track

I am a representative for the Employee Assistance Program (EAP), and I get the greatest satisfaction in seeing American Airlines employees, who have had problems in the past, back on the job and performing well.

I was recently walking in the concourse of one of our larger airports and saw an employee whom I had been able to help more than a decade ago. He had been suffering from serious alcohol abuse problems and was close to losing his job. But because American Airlines is an organization that values our employees and helps them in difficult times, EAP was able to intervene.

We chatted for a while, and he confessed to me that, if American hadn't gotten him the help that he needed, he didn't know whether he would be alive today, much less employed.

As I stood there talking with this healthy, motivated individual, I felt proud to work for a company that treats its employees with the same respect and care with which it treats its customers.

John Tuttle
Employee Assistance Program Representative
Chicago-O'Hare

She Kept Her Promise

During the Vietnam War, our son, John, served in the U.S. Air Force. He had been away a long time, serving at Clark Air Force Base in the Philippines, then Guam and Taiwan, before being sent to Vietnam. After two tours of duty in Vietnam, he was re-assigned to Homestead Air Force Base in Florida. Since we lived in New York at the time, we didn't know when we might see him again.

Apparently, he missed us as much as we all missed him. No one in the family knew, but John had planned a diversion that would get him home for a quick visit before taking his new post. At San Francisco Airport, he checked in on an American flight to New York and asked the ticket agent if she would do him a favor. He told her he wanted to surprise his father and mother when he reached New York. He had hoped to call his brother, Howard, and sister-in-law, Jackie, who lived in Long Island, to meet him at JFK and drive him home to Bronxville, New York. Unfortunately, because of the time difference, both Howard and Jackie were at work, teaching school. The agent promised John that she would keep calling their home until she reached one of them. The agent kept her promise. And, as a result, Howard and Jackie were waiting for John at JFK.

My husband and I will never forget that evening in 1970 when, as we sat down for diner, our doorbell rang. When I answered the door, there were our sons, Howard and John. We hadn't seen John in nearly two years. He quickly picked me up in his arms and hugged me for a very long time. My husband, hearing the commotion and cries of joy, ran to join us.

John never knew the name of the agent that made our homecoming so special. She proved to my family that something as small as following up on a phone call could make a big difference in someone's life. She also made me very proud that I, too, am a part of the American Airlines family.

Isabel W. Hayes
Retired Secretary
Pension & Group Insurance Administration
New York City

When the Call Goes Out, Everyone Answers

Two years ago, my daughter Leslee turned to me for help with a very special task. Leslee heads a nonprofit, non-sectarian group called "Anthony of Padua Gifts for Children." This organization collects toys for inner-city children, some of whom have AIDS, some of whom live in homeless shelters.

In July 1997, Leslee and her volunteers were able to reserve a week at an upstate New York farm for a group of disadvantaged children, four counselors, a lifeguard and a crafts teacher.

She needed help with getting to the farm and obtaining money for all of the expenses. I didn't hesitate for an instant in turning to my colleagues in the American Eagle family for support.

They needed two buses to transport all the children and counselors to camp. Estimates put the cost of each at $1,600. To our rescue came William Buchholz, managing director of American Eagle at JFK. He made a few calls, and Classic Transportation Group provided the group with transportation to and from the farm.

To raise the necessary expense money, Leslee's group decided to hold a raffle. First prize, we determined, had to be special. Again, I turned to American, and asked two of our marketing representatives, Anne Friedman and Sherri Gillette, if they could be of assistance. With an assurance of proper promotion and exposure for American, they were able to obtain two roundtrip tickets anywhere in the United States. It was a grand first prize.

When it came time to sell the raffle tickets, word spread

through the JFK American Eagle station, and agents came in from all departments with offers to help, some to buy and some to sell. The response was overwhelming. Many of our employees who had second jobs even sold their tickets at those other jobs.

I have worked in other companies and other industries, but I've never worked for a company like American. It was this experience that reminded me that the American spirit of loyalty, the American feeling of family, and the American way of giving, are the striking hallmarks of a great company.

John Ferrara
Manager, Catering
New York-Kennedy

Angel Doll

I was a flight attendant onboard the "red-eye" from San Diego to Dallas/Fort Worth five days before Christmas. Carrie, an eight-year-old girl flying with us, was traveling as an unaccompanied minor. Carrie had just been to the funeral of her grandmother, who had raised her from birth, and Carrie was very upset. She seemed so scared and so alone.

I wasn't sure what to do, but for some reason I decided to make an angel doll using one of our travel pillows. I tied a string tight around its middle and used pink towels for wings. Buttons in our sewing kit made perfect eyes and a nose.

I sat down with Carrie and gave her the angel doll. I told her that when she felt upset and scared, to hold her doll close and her grandmother would be with her through her dreams and in her heart. The child fell asleep almost immediately hugging the doll.

Eleven years later, I was working a flight when a young lady came up behind me, tapped me on the shoulder, and asked if I was Jeannie. I said, "Yes." She then handed me a photo of a little girl hugging an angel doll. *She* was Carrie, the little girl in the picture! Carrie told me that she brought the photo with her every time she went to an airport, hoping that some day we would meet again. I was so overwhelmed, I had to fight back tears. Carrie said her doll was her lifeline, and at one time, was her only friend. She was 19 now, and a freshman in college. The other flight attendants saw how emotional I had become; they couldn't believe this reunion could happen!

My reunion with Carrie occurred 14 years ago, and it moved me so much that over the years, flying hundreds of trips, I have made 60 other angel dolls for passengers in distress. I've comforted children and parents who have lost children. Once, I even caught a distraught woman taking an overdose of pills to commit suicide. One of my most emotional moments came when I received a Purple Heart medal in the mail from a woman who had lost her son in the war. I had made her an angel doll, and it meant so much to her that she wanted to share something very important to her with me.

I am so grateful to American Airlines for giving me an opportunity to be a flight attendant and to "attend" to so many wonderful passengers in need.

I am also honored that my angel doll story has been told to newly hired flight attendants at our Learning Center at Dallas/Fort Worth.

Jeannie Wilson
Flight Attendant
Washington

My Dad Would Be Really Proud

When I was nine years old, my father was killed serving in the U.S. Air Force. He was a graduate of astronaut training and had flown 130 missions over North Vietnam in F-105s. His life and early death made such an impact on me that I wanted to fly, just as he did.

After his death, we moved to Dallas to be with family. Over the years, in the hometown of American Airlines, I met many people who worked there. Everyone I knew who worked for American seemed really proud to work there. There seemed to be a sense of family between the workers. While still very young, I vowed to try and become part of that family. All through school I had my sights set on flying and working for American. After serving in the Air Force, I applied for a job and was interviewed by two retired American Airlines captains. Together they asked me a question, "If you were flying with someone you didn't like, how would you handle that?" I thought for a moment, then replied, "Well, I'd have to ask myself why I didn't like the person. If there was no good reason, I might be the one with a problem." Both captains seemed to understand what I meant and laughed. Soon after, I was flying for American. I had become part of the American Airlines family and achieved the goal I had set for myself many, many years ago, after my father's death.

My triumph comes from being a good pilot for American Airlines. I think my dad would be proud that I triumphed over all the difficult times we had without him. And you know, triumph is just a little "umph" added onto "try."

Curtis S. Chastain
Pilot
Dallas/Fort Worth

The FAAmily Helps

I was working in the American Airlines payroll department when my father-in-law died, shortly after the "great flood of Tulsa" in 1984. My in-law's home and business were destroyed by the flood. My mother-in-law, also, had been in very ill health. Our family was devastated.

Upon hearing of our loss, Payroll Manager Jose Falcon took charge, coordinated with Cargo and the funeral home and made *all* the arrangements to transport my father-in-law's body back to Wisconsin for burial. My mother-in-law was adamant that she travel on the same plane as her husband. American arranged it.

It seemed as if every employee we encountered the day we went to Wisconsin was aware of our grief. Our entire family was "cotton-balled" from gate to gate, onboard the aircraft and even at the cargo office in Chicago.

Every obstacle was removed and replaced by gentle and compassionate concern. My heart is still deeply touched by these people, largely strangers, whose only bond with my family was that we were all American Airlines family.

Our greatness as a company comes from within each individual we work with.

Diane Brugger
Passenger Service Agent
New Orleans

I'll Never Fly Another Airline

American Airlines has many firsts in its history in operations, marketing and passenger service. As the industry technology leader, we were the first domestic airline to carry automatic external defibrillators and enhanced medical kits to assist passengers who experience a sudden cardiac arrest or other serious medical problems in flight.

In April 1996, Flight Attendant Susan Wallace had then CEO, Robert Crandall, as a passenger from New York to London. As a recently certified paramedic, she was involved in obtaining automatic external defibrillators for her ambulance service in Warren, Connecticut. During the flight, Ms. Wallace reviewed the values of carrying defibrillators onboard American aircraft and how simple they were to operate with Mr. Crandall. Mr. Crandall took the issue under consideration and two weeks later Ms. Wallace received an invitation to come to Dallas to present the defibrillators to our staff. The first automatic external defibrillators were placed onboard in June 1997.

On February 18, 1998, Shawn Lynn, a flight attendant onboard flight #2017 from Dallas/Fort Worth, saved a passenger's life. When the passenger suffered an obvious heart attack, Shawn instantly started mouth to mouth resuscitation while flight attendant Don Grottman utilized the automated external defibrillator. The passenger was revived.

Nothing reflects the greatness of American Airlines, its attention to the safety and welfare of its customers, and its commitment to excellence, better than these words from the passenger's wife as reflected in her comments to the media:

> For a few minutes, I was a widow. I think if we'd been anywhere else, I'd still be a widow. The flight attendants acted so quickly, it was just amazing. I'll never fly another airline. I don't know why other airlines haven't done this. I mean, I don't care whether we get peanuts or not.

Upgrading our planes to include life saving equipment was not mandated by law. Our company saw the need, trained our crews, and is saving lives. I can't begin to tell you how much I respect American Airlines.

David K. McKenas, M.D. M.P.H.
Corporate Medical Director
Headquarters

Proud To Be an American Airlines Employee

When my parents came to Las Vegas for a visit a few years ago, they were as excited as newlyweds—and that's saying a lot, because they were celebrating their fiftieth wedding anniversary at the time. This goes back a few years, but I'll never forget the story they told about their experience aboard American Airlines.

When my folks checked in for their flight in Cincinnati, my mom casually mentioned to the ticket agent that it was their fiftieth anniversary. The agent simply congratulated them, then directed them to their gate. They never expected what happened next. Upon boarding they were escorted, not to the Main Cabin seats they had purchased, but to First Class where they were offered drinks and a First Class meal. While in the air, the PA system came on and the flight attendant asked for everyone's attention. Boy, were my parents surprised when that "important announcement" turned out to be an anniversary wish from the captain and crew, followed by applause from all the other passengers.

I don't know the names of the employees who brought my parents such happiness, but if they are reading this now, I want to say, "Thank you. You make me proud to be an American Airlines employee."

Fred Gruber
Aircraft Mechanic
Las Vegas

Precious Gift

In 1991 I received a transfer from San Jose, California, to headquarters in Fort Worth, Texas. I wasn't in the position a full week when my father, who was very ill, became critical. Our doctors felt he would pass away within a few hours.

My mom was rushed to the hospital to be with my dad, forgetting to bring my new work number with her. At the hospital she panicked and called American's national toll free number. When the representative asked her what I did, all mom could remember was that I did something to set booking levels for flights.

The reservations agent correctly deduced that I worked somewhere in Yield Management, and with lightning speed he found me, one in 102,900 employees. Within 40 minutes of his call, I was on a plane home.

Because a fellow employee cared enough to find me, I was able to spend a few treasured moments with my dad before he died.

My mom didn't record the reservations agent's name. We have never had the chance to properly thank him for a most precious gift. I believe this story is about what makes our company great and I hope you agree. Perhaps our agent will read it and know how much his extra effort meant to me and my family.

Russell Goutierez
Manager CARE Program, System Operations Control
Flight Academy

Coming Together When Times Are Tough

On any ordinary day, if I were to look up the word "teamwork" in the dictionary it would say: a cooperative effort by the members of a team or group to achieve a common goal. If I were to look up the word "teamwork" after March 8th, 1998, that meaning would hold a lot more truth in my heart.

I had only been flying for four-and-a-half months, was still on probation, and still had the butterflies; all that would not matter on flight #1275.

I had just finished unwrapping all my trays in First Class, when I heard the emergency chime. I opened the cockpit door to find our first officer (a retired AF-AA pilot, 10 years) unconscious. That was where the powerful force of teamwork began with each of us playing a role in our toughest challenge to date. For the next 15 minutes, no questions were asked among myself and my two co-flight attendants, Suze Watson and Lucinda Stroh, as we tried to bring life back to our unconscious colleague; we simply did what we had been trained to do. As three female passengers in the Main Cabin helped prepare the aircraft for landing, miraculously, our captain would bring the plane down from a cruising altitude of 31,000 feet in just six minutes.

The EMT and Life-Flight teams on the ground worked for what seemed like 20 minutes but were unsuccessful. In the end, this man, who had come into our lives just one hour and eight minutes earlier, would be a part of our lives forever.

The team effort extended beyond those on the airplane.

161

Damon Pompa, an AMR-Eagle agent in Lubbock, Texas, ensured every need of the crew and passengers were met, never hesitating for a moment. Thank you to the flight service managers in Ontario, California; Dallas, Texas and Washington D.C., Debbi Luhr from the Association of Professional Flight Attendants and Elise Dzialakiewicz from the Employee Assistance Program. Thank you to everyone—your kind words have helped us all through this hard time.

I am so proud to have had the opportunity to work with my well-trained, quick-thinking, compassionate colleagues, and to work for a company that cares so much for our well-being.

> Ryan Perry
> Flight Attendant
> Washington-Reagan National

Joe Blackwell, a Dallas/Fort Worth-based captain added these words:

Flight attendant, Ryan Perry, a junior employee, traveled all the way from his crew base in Washington, D.C. to speak at the funeral in Texas. He said that although he had only known the first officer for a short time, the incident would have a lasting impact on his own life.

The sense of family at AA transcends a company even as large as American Airlines. Ryan's emotional words were of caring and loss for a departed brother.

What Language Do You Speak?

One of the nice things about American Airlines is that everyone seems to go out of their way to help each other.

I am the uniform coordinator for American Eagle in Dallas. We have employees from many countries and I have a unique opportunity to meet them when they come in for their new uniforms.

To make everyone feel welcome, I began asking employees from various countries to give me a short written phrase in their language to post on the bulletin board in my office.

As new employees come through for their uniforms, it's wonderful to see them smile and remark, "You have my language on your board!"

I have collected 19 languages so far, and eagerly await adding even more. In some small way this makes all of us feel closer to our American family.

Glenda Quick
Uniform Coordinator
American Eagle
Dallas/Fort Worth

Random Acts of Kindness

Sometimes it's the little random acts of kindness that make you realize the world is really full of very fine people.

In January 1995, I encountered one of those fine people, and he was an employee of American Airlines.

As a flight attendant, I had just finished working an exhausting, all-night service from Honolulu to Dallas/ Fort Worth. That morning when we arrived, I was wearing our required Honolulu muumuu uniform, which isn't very warm.

Dallas had just experienced an unexpected cold front and the temperature had plummeted to the low twenties. I stepped off the bus in the employee parking lot—I was very tired and it was bone-chilling cold.

As I walked toward my car I passed an AA employee in a Ground Services uniform and we exchanged "hellos." He obviously recognized that I was exhausted and shivering, and as I began placing my luggage into my car, he appeared at the front of my car with a window scraper.

As I sat in my car trying to get warm, this kind man who didn't know me at all (other than I was a fellow employee), worked methodically to scrape all the frost from all my windows.

I hope you publish my letter because I would like everyone to know about the wonderful people who work for our company. Thank you.

Patricia Grace
Flight Attendant
Dallas/Fort Worth

164

We Have Amazing Members in Our Family!

I am an American Airlines passenger service agent in Toronto. I was traveling on vacation to Mexico City and had to transfer in Chicago to my Mexico flight. Our inbound flight was late and I only had about six minutes to connect from the end of one concourse to the front of another. As I was racing to catch my flight, I realized I had taken my grandmother's engagement ring off my hand, carefully placed it in the empty seat next to me, and then promptly forgot about it! The ring is invaluable to me. I didn't know what to do. I stopped running and asked the first gate agent I came to for help. She called the inbound gate and in a moment said, "We have your ring!" I gave her my name and phone number in Toronto and begged her to do everything possible to get my ring to me before my flight to Mexico departed.

Just as the bridge was about to pull back, an agent sprinted up to the flight attendant and I was paged to the front of the aircraft to claim my ring.

The agents in Chicago were amazing. It's because of co-workers like this that I am so very proud to be a part of the American Airlines family.

Leigh McCrodan
Passenger Service
Toronto

Where There's a Will, There's a Way

After 22 years as a single parent, Joanne was to be married. Her oldest daughter, Wendy, was the matron of honor—plans were finalized months in advance.

Wendy and her husband, John, were to fly to California from New York. On the day of their departure, a severe snow storm closed all of the New York metropolitan airports, canceling all flights.

Determined to be present at her mom's wedding, Wendy and her husband drove from their home in Yorktown Heights, New York, through New Jersey, to Pennsylvania, where they could catch a flight to Dallas, and then connect to a Los Angeles flight. Despite all of their efforts, the long drive and connecting flights made it impossible for the couple to arrive in time for the 4 p.m. West Coast ceremony.

Not ready to give up, the family arranged for a speakerphone to be set up at the church so that the minister and wedding party could communicate with Wendy over the airplane's in-flight phone.

All the passengers on the plane followed the excitement, and when the service was finished, the entire plane cheered.

A very grateful Wendy and her mom said, "Thank you, American, for coming through for us."

Excerpts from *Flagship News* July 4, 1994

American's Lessons

I worked for American Airlines for 20 years. When my husband, Victor, retired, we decided to relocate to Florida where we both became involved in volunteer work. The service philosophy inculcated from my years at American—understanding each customer's needs and zeroing in on their problems—translated easily into our work, conducting workshops for volunteers with the homeless, migrants, immigrants, and people who had made poor life choices.

Mr. Crandall's and Mr. Carty's letter regarding *A Spirit of Greatness* arrived just two days prior to Victor's passing away. At his wake, many of the less fortunate people we helped came to pay their respects.

My participation in your book would be a tribute to Victor. I thank American Airlines for the training I received that allowed Victor and me to help so many in need.

Rosemary (Rory) Cangro
Retired Sales Agent
New York-Kennedy

Important Message

November 25, 1997

Dear Captain C.D. Ewell,

Today is the third day of my first three-day trip in three-and-a-half months. Four months ago, a doctor told me I had throat cancer. A second opinion at the Mayo Clinic confirmed the first. Eleven days in the hospital, three cancer operations on my throat, and thirty radiation treatments ended one month ago. And now, after a month, I am back on the line.

As I think about the blessings in my life, my family and their support are number one. But the support of my fellow pilots and the Chicago flight office was overwhelming.

Now I am back to normal. And it is great! I just wish I could tell my fellow crew members two things:

First, the company cancer screening is an excellent program. Please encourage everyone to use it.

Second, I was in the dumps with the radiation treatment, but I kept thinking about how great it is to be part of American Airlines. Keeping that in mind, it was easy to have a positive attitude and strive to return to the greatest job in the world!

Captain Jon Cichucki

Editor's Note: In June 1998 Captain Cichucki happily reported that he is cancer-free and doing well.

It Could Have Been *My* Father

That's what always crosses my mind when I help an older passenger. On a recent flight from Aruba to New York, one of our passengers was an elderly man who could not get around by himself. As I completed my cabin walk-through, he stopped me and very shyly asked me (as the only male attendant on the flight) to take him to the bathroom. It was a simple request, but I could see he had summoned up all his courage to make it.

I was happy to assist him, because every time I come across a situation like this, I think of my father. That thought gives me all the enthusiasm I need to help older people. In fact, I think it's a pleasure to be able to do something for an older person because I know that one day I may well be in the same situation.

Javier A. Urena
Flight Attendant
New York-Kennedy

My Angel

It was Christmas, and I was working. I really wanted to be with my family, and I was having a "low" moment.

I finished my shift, gathered up my tickets and papers, and proceeded down the long, empty concourse to the agent control center. There was no doubt about it, I was feeling sorry for myself, being alone on Christmas day. I dropped one of my tickets, and was bending over to pick it up, when I saw a young girl walking directly toward me. Her eyes were glistening with tears, and she looked as sad as I felt. She told me she had missed her last chance to get home for Christmas.

I heard myself saying, "Come on, let's check again." I was able to find a connection to her destination so that she could arrive home that day. The girl was so grateful that she gave me a large tin of homemade candy, and I think that made us both feel good.

A year later on Christmas day, that same young lady approached me again at my gate, extended her hand and asked, "Remember me? I just wanted to thank you again."

To this day, I believe she appeared "from nowhere" when I was feeling especially sorry for myself. Maybe she was an angel, but whatever she was, she gave me the lift I needed to remind me how important it was to help other people, especially during the holidays.

Jan Hoyng
Retired Passenger Service Agent
Dayton, Sacramento, Raleigh/Durham

Take Care of My Baby

Early one morning, a few months ago, the co-pilot and I walked up to the window at our departure gate confirming what I already knew—the day wasn't starting well. The rain that had soaked us at the hotel was still coming down hard. I saw through the rain that the jetbridge wasn't yet attached to our plane. This, after a ride to the airport with a teenage driver subjecting us to loud music that rang through our half-asleep brains. And the hotel coffee's only redeeming qualities were that it was free and hadn't spilled during the Indy-like sprint to the airport.

"Why do we do this?" the co-pilot asked, shaking his head as he set down his kit bag and walked away.

As I watched the inactivity on the airport ramp, my thoughts turned back to a small Florida airstrip. The movie that played in my mind was of my first solo. My stomach tightened as I remembered the combination of fear and exhilaration which had left me unable to sleep the night before. Just as I broke ground, any doubt was washed away by the thrill of being alone in the air. Time stood still as I climbed slowly upward. As I flew past the lone airport building, I could see my parents standing outside. My father was too stoic to join in my mother's enthusiastic waving, but I knew he had a smile just as wide as my own. Even though I was only a teenager, I knew then that flying was what I would do for the rest of my life.

My memories moved several years forward as I now

stood behind my Air Force cargo airplane that slowly gave up its huge load to the waiting hands of people in need. We'd been called to this country, recently wracked by an earthquake that had claimed over 100,000 victims. Television pictures couldn't fully capture the devastation and despair. Usually large machines unloaded this aircraft, but there were no such machines here and many of the victims formed a huge bucket brigade. They passed 60,000 pounds of cargo by hand—one small box at a time—along the line to waiting trucks. Their look of tired determination told the entire story. Our airplane had brought hope and a chance at life. It was these times when mine wasn't just another job.

I was pulled from my thoughts by the sound of laughter in the departure lounge. A couple stood near me with their teenage son, the father and mother each hugging the boy. The mother spoke unheard words, kissed the boy lightly on the cheek and then straightened as her husband circled her shoulder with his arm. The father looked over at me and smiled broadly.

"Our son's flying off to college. You going to be the pilot?' he asked.

"Yes sir," I said.

As the woman turned to me, she wiped away tears. "Take care of my baby," she said.

I smiled and nodded my agreement as they shared some last-minute time together. I turned back to the terminal window. The sun was just starting to peek over the horizon. The rain-covered ramp glistened with the cleanliness of a new day. The co-pilot returned.

"Here, boss." He handed me a fresh cup of coffee. "You look a million miles away," he said.

I took a sip of the coffee and looked over at the family. "Nah, just remembering why we do this."

Don Dillman
Captain
Flight Academy
Headquarters

A Great Adventure

Dear American,

My son was traveling as an unaccompanied minor on another airline. His flight was canceled and he was transferred to American. The American flight was subsequently canceled due to bad weather. Chicago-based Captain Barr McCutcheon and First Officer Tim Bradley spotted my distressed child and took charge. They contacted me with my son's new flight information, took him to dinner, and let him stay with them at the crew hotel. They escorted him to his flight the next day and Captain McCutcheon called to ensure my son was home safely. These two pilots turned a parent's worst nightmare into a great adventure for my son.

Sincerely,
M.P.
Springfield, Illinois

Flagship News, April 3, 1995

Service Continues Beyond the Airport

I am carrying on the third generation of aviation in my family, two of which are with American Airlines. My father is a pilot, his father, a 32-year veteran of American Airlines, and myself going on 11 years. We are loyal to American Airlines for many reasons.

One of them is that the company believes that service to the community is as important as service to the customer.

In Tulsa, an A&P mechanic is allowed to help with children and the elderly at St. Francis Hospital. This practice is because we have very supportive bosses, Brian Bricken and Joe DeLustro.

My volunteer work is in music therapy, and while there, everyone seems to forget their problems as we have fun with puppetry, singing and playing instruments. I believe this helps quicken their recovery.

Everyone hears about American Airlines each week and, although they want me to stay longer, I tell them that it's important that I get back on the job and do my part working on the engines for the planes.

"I hope I don't see you next week," I tell them. I'd much rather see them boarding a flight for a vacation.

T.J. Manchester
A&P Mechanic
Tulsa

Special Delivery

Dear American,

As an Air Force pilot, I'm often separated from my family.

Recently, I was in Little Rock for military training. My wife was at home, pregnant with our first child. I received a call from her saying that she was in labor.

I took the earliest flight possible that evening on American. En route to Seattle, a flight attendant awakened me and explained that the flight crew had received a message alerting them to my wife's condition. She told me to move to the front of the First Class cabin so I could deplane quickly. I happily accepted and took my place in the front.

The jetbridge had barely reached the door of the plane when I was greeted by a uniformed employee, waiting to meet "the expectant father." To cheers of "congratulations!" and "good luck!" from the flight crew, we sprinted to the gate entrance where an electric cart was waiting. We reached the terminal door, and my waiting ride, in record time.

I arrived at the hospital at 1:15 a.m., and my wife delivered our daughter 15 minutes later. I'm convinced that without the special attention and superb assistance provided by your staff, I wouldn't have been there in time.

Thanks to airport operations agents, Charnita Boyd and Colleen Jackson, who alerted the crew and assisted me at the gate, and to the flight crew and all those who helped behind the scenes. They helped me witness a miracle.

A.D.B.
Tacoma, Washington

Excerpts from *Flagship News,* November 28, 1994

Showing Concern for Passengers

I recently was traveling with my two small children from Dallas/Fort Worth to Cleveland. After we had boarded, the plane had mechanical problems.

After about two hours, the passengers were allowed to deplane and make phone calls. Because my two children were sleeping, I chose to stay onboard. Suddenly, a young man appeared, introduced himself as an off-duty AA pilot, and offered me his credit card to make a call from the in-flight telephone.

I know he had no idea that I was a fellow employee. Perhaps he had small children himself and understood my situation. Whatever his motivation, he saw someone who needed help and he lent a hand. I declined his generous offer and thanked him for his concern.

I've thought about this incident a number of times, because I think this person exemplifies the American Airlines spirit of putting the customer first. That pilot's actions have certainly inspired me in my service to our customers.

Mary (Laptiuk) Pierce
Flight Attendant
Dallas/Fort Worth

Wake-Up Call

I think we all get jaded sometimes, going through the motions of everyday life. But life has a way of sending a wake-up call, and somehow things never seem the same again. That's what happened when I met the Johnsons. Mrs. Johnson was at my desk, asking if she could get seat assignments. Mr. Johnson had a tired look about his face, as if life had not been kind to him. When I told Mrs. Johnson that check-in would begin in about 10 minutes, she gave me such a warm smile, and said, "Okay. Thank you. I'll come back." She looked at me, sadly, as though she needed to talk. Due to my own grief (my mother had passed away recently), I sensed that I should not pressure her in any way.

A few minutes later, Mrs. Johnson returned to my counter and asked if I could enroll her husband in the AAdvantage program. She said that, although she knew that this would be his last trip, she wanted him to think otherwise. I said, "Yes, of course. I will sign him up." I looked over at Mr. Johnson. Seeing him brought back all the excruciating pain I had felt as I watched my own mother waste away during her final stages of cancer, and I began to cry. I said, "Mrs. Johnson, if you don't mind my asking, what is wrong with your husband?" She replied, "He has pancreatic cancer," which confirmed what I had feared.

As Mrs. Johnson explained to me that her husband did not have much time left, she, too, began to cry and we hugged. I told her about losing my mother to cancer the previous year and about how it still hurt. Then I walked over to Mr. Johnson and said, "Hello. My name is Mari-anne. If there's anything that you need, or anything I can do for you, please don't hesitate to ask me." Mr. Johnson sat silently, and as I touched his hand, he nodded his head.

Back at the counter, where Mrs. Johnson was still stand-ing, she told me that she had lost so many loved ones to cancer, including her father and first husband. Suddenly, she cried out, "This is just not fair!" I was so deeply moved by Mrs. Johnson, that I started to cry uncontrol-lably. The agent working with me had to take over the flight, while Mrs. Johnson and I tried to hide our emotions from her husband.

I called my supervisor and explained the situation. I asked if I could upgrade the Johnsons. Being just as touched as I was, he advised me to give them First Class treatment. The First Class cabin was open, so I upgraded them on their flight from Chicago to Newark, and through to San Juan, where they were taking a seven-day cruise to the Bahamas. As I gave Mrs. Johnson the boarding passes, I said, "I hope this makes the trip more pleasur-able for the two of you."

Walking back to the counter, I thought of my own mom and how she prayed to return to San Juan to see her mother before she died. The tears ran from my eyes as I remem-bered how mom had died right before she was to take her trip. Knowing that this would likely be Mr. Johnson's last trip, I asked myself, "What else can I do for him?" Think-ing of my mother and the trip she never got to take, I ran to the computer and upgraded the Johnsons to First Class for their return trip from San Juan.

Once the Johnsons were boarded and settled in, I went

onboard and explained to them that they were upgraded to First Class on all of their flights. From the bottom of my heart, I wished these lovely people, who had touched my life as no one else could, the best.

A month later, I received a letter from the Johnsons telling me how magnificent their trip had been, and how what I had done for them had made it the vacation of their dreams. I felt so good to know that I had helped.

On December 28th, I received another letter, which was written by Mrs. Johnson on Christmas Eve, telling me that on December 6th, her birthday, Mr. Johnson had passed away.

The news was devastating. I thought about Mrs. Johnson's courage. It was so amazing to me. Knowing how much she hurt, yet still managed to smile, reminded me of my mother. Mrs. Johnson made me see that life goes on. I thought to myself, "Keep your head up, Mrs. Johnson. We are going to make it."

Marianne Benitez
Passenger Service Agent
Chicago-O'Hare

We Can Make a Difference

While I was a flight attendant, as often happens, my one-day trip was reassigned as a three-day trip. I wasn't a happy camper. With bad weather en route, the captain cancelled our beverage service, and I decided to head to the back of the plane and feel sorry for myself. On the way, I saw a young mother with a beautiful new baby boy. He was irresistible—I had to stop and hold him. His name was Logan, and he was the most beautiful, alert infant I had ever seen. During my conversation with his mom, I learned that Logan had Downs Syndrome.

The 40-minute flight seemed to fly by, leaving me in a good mood. After landing, Logan's mom walked by my jump seat. As she approached, I noticed that she was crying. To my surprise she came up to me and gave me a huge hug and thanked me. She told me that usually, when she tells people that Logan has Downs Syndrome, people hand him back to her like he has some contagious disease. She went on to say that even her own mother did. My heart went out to the two of them. I told her again how wonderful her baby was and took him in my arms and personally helped them off the plane.

I have always remembered this experience because it shows that American Airlines front line employees really can make a difference in the lives of others—even when you don't set out to do it. We care, and our customers are richer because of it.

Chip Wood
Administrator, AAdvantage Marketing Programs
Headquarters

Looking Out for Each Other

I'm an American Airlines employee and I am still overwhelmed by the generosity and caring of my fellow employees. Here's an example of what I mean:

I was in Chicago when another flight attendant accidentally carried off my tote bag. With three days of the trip left, I was obviously upset to be without money and clothes. To make matters worse, when we completed the first leg of the trip and arrived in Dallas/Fort Worth, a supervisor met my flight to inform me that I had a family emergency and should call home immediately. I learned that my sister was seriously ill and had been taken to the hospital. Within minutes of hanging up the phone, I was rushing to my next gate. Out of breath, I explained all that had just happened and the distressing news from home to the gate agent.

Once onboard, I made my way to the back galley and was surprised to see that the agent had followed me there. He handed me his business card and told me he would be happy to do whatever he could to help my situation, then turned and left the plane. When I flipped the business card over, I was stunned to find a $100 bill stapled to the back! I quickly tried to catch up with him to return his money, but he was nowhere in sight. Later, another agent told me that his co-worker said he just wanted to do something to make my day better than it had started out. This man's generosity and thoughtfulness touched me—after all, we had never met before. It's people like him that make American great.

Bridgette Gilchrist
Flight Attendant
Chicago-O'Hare

The Stuff We're Made Of

We all know that American employees do a great job when they are being paid, but I'd like to mention two examples of wonderful qualities exhibited when employees are *not* being paid.

A while ago, my wife and I returned from a trip to find our car battery dead. I spotted a man walking into the parking lot. He happened to be an AA employee. Before I had identified myself as a fellow employee, he quickly offered us assistance, pulled his car next to ours, attached a set of battery cables and got us on our way home. When I contacted the airport manager to commend the employee for going out of his way, the manager noted that this employee had received numerous accolades and commendations for helping customers.

A second example occurred just recently. My sister lives in a distant city and became seriously ill. I was greatly concerned for her health and decided to try to reach a fellow employee (my first instructor in Reservations forty years ago!) who happened to live in my sister's hometown. While I had not spoken to this employee in many years, she was quick to help. She went out of her way to contact my sister and even arranged for her local church to provide additional support.

These are just two examples of so many that come to mind about fellow employees who do great things, even for people they don't know, especially when they don't have to. I think this is what makes our company great!

Charlie Zimmerli
Retired Division Manager, Reservations
Hartford

Caring for All of Our Passengers

The dog days of August had really made their mark on the tarmac at O'Hare. It was blistering hot, and the freight from a flight from Detroit was off-loaded and brought across the field in metal carts. One connecting shipment contained a trained border patrol dog, destined for San Antonio. The flight was several hours away, and the freight clerks placed the kennel where a breeze might ease the dog's confinement.

On this particular aluminum kennel, the trough was corroded, and it could not be pulled out to give the dog some water. Knowing that the animal was going to be uncomfortable during its long wait, I went to the lunchroom and found a soft drink bottle, which I washed out and filled with cold water. I took it to the kennel and let the dog smell the refreshing, cold water. I gave some firm commands—back, sit. She obeyed, and I flattened a styrofoam cup and pushed it through the bars. I then formed the cup back into shape and poured water into it. "Come," I said. She drank, and with each lap of her tongue, brushed against my finger. I kept pouring the water as she drank.

"Good dog," I said. Later, each time as I passed the kennel, her eyes followed my every move. Perhaps she was saying "thank you."

Now, this dog was never going to write a letter of commendation to American Airlines' senior management. No one was going to know that my colleagues and I in Freight Services attempted to make her stay with us a bit more comfortable. But the AA motto that the customer comes first extends to *all* passengers. Could I have done anything less?

Ann Rose Bartik
Retired Freight Claims Agent
Chicago-O'Hare

Small Efforts Bring Big Dividends

Recently I was welcoming an elderly couple aboard who were pre-boarding our aircraft. The gentleman, making his way with some difficulty and the aid of a crutch, stopped momentarily to look into the cockpit. His wife explained that her husband was a private pilot and an aviation enthusiast. I invited them to come up into the cockpit for a closer look after we had arrived at our destination and the other passengers had de-planed. On arrival, the husband eagerly moved into the captain's seat and was given a guided tour by my first officer. In the galley, the gentleman's wife explained to me that her husband had terminal bone cancer and that this may very well be his last flight. After several minutes of conversation the couple graciously thanked us and headed for baggage claim . . . his spirits noticeably uplifted.

Watching them leave, my spirits were uplifted as well. I was reminded that the small effort required to take a personal interest in others can pay big dividends and be very rewarding.

David Krueger
Captain
Dallas/Fort Worth

Thanks for Looking after My Wife

I'm a mechanic, and while working in Houston, I received a routine call from a 727 flight engineer to fix a loose bolt on a panel in the wheel well. I tightened the bolt, checked for any other problems and returned to the office.

Later, I was walking through the terminal, and an older gentleman approached me. He had a big smile on his face and extended his hand.

"I want to thank you," he said.

"What for?" I asked, shaking his hand.

"I was looking out the terminal window and saw you tightening that bolt on the 727 the other day," he answered. "My wife was on that flight. Thanks for taking care of her."

As he walked away, a powerful feeling of satisfaction came over me. I really did take care of his wife, and that man made me feel very proud.

Doug Cardwell
Mechanic/Tay Shop
Alliance Maintenance Base

More Than a Labor of Love

When 21-year-old Sandra Robledo went into labor over the Pacific on a Tokyo-to-Seattle flight, en route to Cali, Colombia, she was alone, spoke no English and thought she was friendless.

Thanks to several caring AAers, she found that she was wrong on the final point.

Because of their efforts to help the traveler, four Seattle-based flight attendants—LaMonte Evans and his wife, Ola, along with Karen Bauer, and Keiko Shirakata—recently received "Customer Comes First" awards. Agents Joanna Chaparro and Helena Tanoura also earned praise for their compassion.

During the three hours before the flight could reach Seattle, LaMonte Evans, assisted by Bauer and Shirakata, helped the passenger relax by teaching her breathing techniques.

When the aircraft finally landed, Evans and agent Chaparro, a native of Colombia who could handle translations, accompanied Robledo to the hospital. There, with Bauer and Shirakata also in attendance, she promptly delivered a new U.S. citizen—a daughter she named Hemely.

Over the next couple of days, the new mother received flowers, baby clothes and other gifts from the Evans, from agents Chaparro and Tanoura, who helped with translations, and other AA well-wishers.

Barbara Vann, director of the Highline Family Childbirth Center, would later express her staff's "surprise and pleasure" at the concern Seattle AAers demonstrated.

But Robledo's troubles weren't over. Since she was traveling without a visa, she faced the prospect of spending a week in a hotel—with a guard—until she was medically able to fly on to Colombia.

Determined not to let that happen, Flight Service Base Manager Linda Roundtree secured approval from headquarters to take the new mother and child into her home. She received help from the Evanses, who visited every day.

Meanwhile, General Manager Bob Johnson, reported Seattle's "Team Narita" had been busy, working with the Immigration and Naturalization Service to secure a temporary visa.

International Departure Coordinator Anne Grove was able to obtain a birth certificate for the infant overnight, rather than waiting the customary 30 days. That allowed the baby—a U.S. citizen by virtue of birth in this country— to be issued a U.S. passport in just under 48 hours so she could fly to Colombia with her mother a week later.

Excerpts from Flagship News March 23, 1998

Magical Moments

A few years ago, on a Friday night flight to Denver, a passenger asked the flight attendants if we could do him a favor. The young man's girlfriend was meeting him at the airport in Denver and he was planning to propose to her. He had brought with him 99 long stem red roses and one long stem white rose. Nestled between the petals of the single white rose was an engagement ring. He wanted 99 passengers to deplane before him, each handing his girlfriend a red rose. He would come out last carrying the white rose with the ring and propose to her. We made an announcement explaining this gentleman's plan and asked for volunteers. Everyone wanted to be a part of the romantic event! Throughout the flight the young man went through the cabin showing the engagement ring and receiving congratulations. The warm wishes and feeling of joy were overwhelming.

When we arrived in Denver the passengers deplaned and the crew followed our Romeo out of the jetbridge. There, under a mountain of roses, we found Juliet and a plane full of passengers patiently waiting to spy on this special moment. Romeo took the roses from his soon-to-be bride's arms, laid them on a chair, dropped to one knee and professed his love for her as he handed her his single white rose. Through her tears she said "Yes!" and the audience broke into cheers. Cameras flashed and best wishes were given. It was one of those many magical moments and I was so proud to be a part of it.

Jill LaBoy
Flight Attendant
San Francisco

Lending a Hand

For some, retirement means relaxing and enjoying a slower pace of life. For Jack Despins, after 30 years of service for American Airlines, he's not about to slow down.

These days, Jack fills his time with volunteer work for his church that includes delivering food for the HOPE (Helping Other People Everywhere) program, recycling cans for the Meals on Wheels program and performing odd jobs, such as transporting donated furniture.

Jack also manages to incorporate his association with American Airlines in a very creative way.

Last fall, Jack and his son salvaged 6,000 pounds of discarded airline seat fabric that Jack is now giving new life. In his garage workshop, on a contraption of his own design, Jack cuts and sews the fabric into blankets for the homeless. To date, he has made over 200 blankets and is still going strong. Although he donates the blankets to the Salvation Army for distribution to the homeless, Jack always makes sure he has one blanket in the back of his truck—just in case he can ever lend a hand.

Editor

The Bionic Man

I think I am living proof of what happens when a person's life is positively affected by his job. If he really likes, or in my case, loves his work, it can impact his entire existence.

I am an aircraft mechanic for American Airlines based in Miami. A number of years ago I was diagnosed with acute leukemia. We had just purchased our first home, and my daughter was only eighteen months old. My entire world was falling apart.

I went through intense chemotherapy and survived. I really believe the support of my family and my colleagues at American, coupled with my strong desire to rejoin my team at American, helped me through my illness.

Five years later, I had another attack of leukemia, which I again beat. I've also had to deal with other related medical problems—hip surgery and a liver transplant, but I've always come through. My co-workers at American call me the "Bionic Man."

American is great for many reasons. In my case, it's because the company and the employees gave me the loyalty, friendship and strength that I needed to overcome my personal challenges.

Jeffrey P. Henderson
Maintenance
Miami

The Brightest Time of My Life

At age 50, I was out of a job and flat broke. I had my wife, Dorothy, and four young daughters to support. I was offered a job as a fleet service clerk at JFK. It turned my whole life around. Giving me a chance to prove myself and help my family is what I think makes American great. Working at American has been the brightest time of my life. I know American is the best airline in the world, and that gives me great pride.

Arthur H. Earle
Retired Fleet Service Clerk, Cabin Service
New York-Kennedy

WORDS OF WISDOM

Resilience

My father, Walter Murphy, gave me some of the best advice I've ever received and it has helped me through some of my most difficult times.

He told me resilience is the key to being successful. The ability to bounce back, never give up, and view setbacks simply as lessons, not failures—that's how you get ahead.

I've lived my life remembering my dad's advice and it really works. No matter if it's providing the finest in flight service or working my way through life's challenges, it works.

Deborah C. Benker
International Purser, Flight Attendant
San Francisco

Increase Your Revenue the Easy Way

Providing great service to your customers doesn't always translate into extra costs for the company. In fact, sometimes it translates into major increases in new business and usually, it only requires a little extra effort on your part, along with a little ingenuity.

Years ago, the chairman of one of American's largest corporate accounts was giving a speech in Scottsdale, Arizona. His company's travel manager had called us to arrange V.I.P. treatment for him at the airport. During the conversation, I asked about special handling for his golf clubs. The travel manager told me the chairman was not bringing his clubs—too much effort for only one round of golf. My immediate reaction was, "What a great opportunity for American to look good, and for us to make the travel manager look good."

I had the travel manager contact the chairman's doorman at his apartment in New York City. We sent a sales representative to his building, up to his apartment, took his clubs from the closet, out to the airport, and into the cargo compartment of a Phoenix flight. Another sales representative in Phoenix met the flight, picked up the clubs, and brought them to the country club. When the chairman walked out on the first tee thinking he was using rentals, we handed him his own clubs. He could not believe it. At the 18th hole, our representative collected the clubs, returned them to the airport and loaded them on a New York inbound. In New York, we collected the clubs again, brought them back to his apartment, and returned them to the closet.

From that day on, we "owned" this account. The chairman even used this story at his annual management meeting where he discussed customer service. Following this very simple display of concern, American took over the logistics of their sales meetings, training seminars and became the chairman's (and travel manager's) preferred airline. Our revenue almost doubled.

John M. Capozzi

Look What I Started!

"I try to treat every customer as though they owned the company."

Mark Hawkins
Reservations Agent
Dallas

I Give Them My Best

Over the years, I have learned to recognize the newcomers to flying. As a flight attendant, I've learned to see and hear things from the passenger's perspective. The newcomers are nervous and unsure of their surroundings. I try to put myself in their shoes. Sounds that are routine to the crew can be pretty alarming for some passengers. With imaginations working overtime, I guess an air conditioning jet could sound like the cabin depressurizing, and the sound of the main landing gear coming down prior to final approach can really be awesome to a newcomer. A little bit of understanding goes a long way. I've met some pretty amazing newcomers throughout my career and I hope they walk away thinking that they've met one of American's finest, because I always try to give them my best. If I can make one newcomer feel at ease on my flight, then I'm doing one of the things I was hired to do.

Debra Field
Flight Attendant
New York-Kennedy

. . . And I Mean It!

My job description doesn't include customer relations work, but at American Airlines, we're told that every employee has an obligation to assist customers at all times.

As a line avionics mechanic, I am called upon to respond to last minute checks on the aircraft. Seeing me in the cockpit often prompts passengers to ask if the airplane is "safe."

My standard reply always reassures them; "This is American Airlines. If there's any doubt about this plane, it will stay here at JFK and American will put all the passengers on another plane."

And I mean it.

Eve Stewart
Line Avionics Mechanic
New York-Kennedy

You Never Get a Second Chance to Make a Good First Impression

First impressions are the ones that last. So the first thing any customer sees when they approach my desk is a big smile. I want them to feel relaxed and confident that I can help them get to and from their destinations safely and easily. A smile says you care and that you're happy to serve them. I've only been an American Airlines employee for a short time, but I'm the happiest I've ever been in any job. And I think it shows.

Mary Ann McCaffrey
Customer Service Agent
Chicago-O'Hare

We Make the Right Decisions

As an instructor, I always tell my students that the most important thing they can do when they are flying is to imagine that the people they love the most are on the flight. If they will do that, they will always make the right decisions.

Dennis Risinger
Instructor
American Eagle Training Center
Headquarters

Kind Words

It was only after the birth of my daughter, and the death of my father six months later, that I realized how much hearing the words, "Congratulations" and "I'm sorry" can mean.

Since then, whenever a passenger flies with us, be it for a joyous or sorrowful occasion, I try to say a little something to acknowledge their situation. I think our own life events make us better people and better employees.

Lori Duenhoft
International AAdvantage Reservations Agent/
Senior Sales & Service
Washington-Dulles

Our Main Goals

Despite differences in cultures, ideals, and egos, our crew always comes together for two common goals: keeping our aircraft safe for our passengers, and keeping the "On-Time Machine" on time. That's what being a great airline is all about.

Mike Zelsnack
Crew Chief
Tulsa

Look to Your Own First to Solve a Problem

Almost twenty years ago, when I was a welder in our engine shop, I was asked to design a special stand for our inspectors to use during engine inspections. The stand that I made worked so well that I was asked to make others—and these stands are still used today. I am very honored that I was able to create something that worked well for my company, saved people lots of time and allowed inspectors to do a better job. I am equally impressed that our company had the confidence to turn to one of its own to solve this problem.

Fred Roberts
Retired Aircraft Mechanic and Welder
Los Angeles

The Customer is the Boss

Sam Walton once said:

"There is only one boss: the customer. And he can fire everybody in the company, from the chairman on down, simply by spending his money somewhere else."

I try to follow this maxim every day.

John Newfield
Manager, Tulsa Warehouse Operations
Materials Management
Tulsa

We Learn from Our Customers

We can often learn valuable lessons from our customers.

An incident many years ago molded my career, and I'm grateful for the experience. I had an early morning shift in Reservations, and I arrived not in the best of moods. I was on the phone with a passenger, and he apparently detected my bad mood.

Suddenly, he said, "May I have my seat with a smile, please?"

That statement straightened out my attitude, real quick!

His simple reminder stayed with me through more than 25 years with American. I have told this story many times in team meetings and have even used it with some sales clerks.

This reminder has served me well over the years. I have many letters of appreciation from passengers and a framed letter from former Chairman Bob Crandall for my work in customer service.

Joyce L. Engel
Retired International Sales Representative
Cincinnati

Start off with a Laugh

"So, how are you doing today?"

As a world tariff agent who interacts daily with reservations agents, ticket counter agents and travel agents, I must get asked this question hundreds of times daily.

I always try to reply in a way that I know will put a smile on the faces of the men and women on the front line:

"I'm a shade shy of perfect," or, "If I were any better, I'd be swimming in a pool of Margaritas," starts our conversation off with a burst of laughter . . . they feel better, and it makes me feel great.

Rita A. Jackson
World Tariff Agent
Southern Reservations Office
Dallas/Fort Worth

We All Have an Opportunity

I started with American as a cabin cleaner, and today, I'm a ticket agent. Every American employee has the opportunity for advancement. If an employee applies him or herself and strives to offer the best of their abilities to the company for one common goal—pleasing and accommodating the customers in a professional manner—they'll have the opportunity to grow with the company.

I try to do the best job that I can every day, representing AA in a positive way, so we all can prosper as a company, while prospering individually.

Doloris "Robbie" Artis
Ticket Agent
Los Angeles

We Don't Need Any Unhappy Passengers

A happy passenger tells maybe one other person. An unhappy passenger is eager to tell at least ten—that's nine good reasons to try your best.

V. Rescigno
Special Services Associate
Los Angeles

Keep the Door Open for Better Communication

As a captain, it's important for me to make contact with the passengers on each flight by doing more than just making announcements while we're en route.

I always open the cockpit door when the passengers are deplaning. It gives them a chance to stop by and say hello or comment on the flight.

One thing I have noticed over the years is that you can easily tell the way the passengers have been treated by the flight attendants by their comments as they deplane. Those occasions when the passengers have had the most pleasant experience are when the cabin crew has been friendly, energetic and enthusiastic.

These traits ensure not only repeat customers, but a positive work environment for all.

Dennis Wilkins
Captain
Los Angeles

Be the Best That You Can Be

A positive attitude is everything at American. So I developed a little affirmation to help me stay focused on being positive each day; "I am the best that I can be" was my trademark line. Occasionally, problems came up, but I have always found that my attitude was instrumental in relieving the stress of the situation and putting people at ease.

J.W. Robertson
Retired Quality Assurance Supervisor
Tulsa

Family

For the past nine years I have flown our Chicago-Stockholm route. It's a popular route, and it's always booked. As you'd expect, we have many frequent flyers and repeat customers. After nine years of flying an eight and a half-hour flight, you get to know most of them very well. My passengers know me by name and vice versa. If we run out of something onboard, the First Class, Business Class, or Main Cabin crew will help each other. We consider our passengers and crew family and that's why it all works so well. That's why so many of our customers keep coming back . . . we've become part of their family too.

Anna Winship
Flight Attendant
Los Angeles

ON THE LIGHTER SIDE

"She *Told* Me to Take It"

Some years ago, a deplaning passenger approached my wife, an American ticket agent in Philadelphia. He asked, "How do I get to downtown Philadelphia?" Elaine replied, "Just go outside and take one of the limousines."

That's exactly what he did. Really impressed with our service, he got behind the wheel of a "limo" and drove off. The police intercepted him about half-way to downtown.

Elaine never used that particular phrase again and *Air Transport World* magazine ran the story.

Robert C. Dick
Retired Director
Flight Claims Administration
Headquarters

Total Commitment

I think the single most important factor that makes American Airlines a great company is its total commitment to the needs of its customers, regardless of their nature or magnitude.

I remember a situation I was involved in as a new hire on probation.

I was a flight engineer. We had begun our descent into Boston when a flight attendant informed me that a lady in First Class was deeply concerned for the well-being of her dog traveling in the baggage compartment. Wanting to make a proper impression as a new employee, and wanting to be a part of this amazing American Airlines history of great passenger service, I volunteered to retrieve the dog and personally deliver it in good condition to our passenger.

Upon arrival I went down to the cargo compartment only to find the dog lying in its cage with no visible signs of life. Here I was, my first opportunity to make a positive impression on everyone as a flight crew member for American Airlines, and the dog was dead! This lady was sure to blame me for the demise of her dog. I could see incident reports being sent to senior management everywhere.

Suddenly, the dog opened one eye. It was alive! My only thought was to quickly get the dog to the lady while there still existed a breath of life.

I literally ran up the jetbridge into the aircraft—no lady. I ran down the concourse towards the baggage claim area—no lady. As I ran through the terminal trying to hold the cage as steady as possible, dodging oncoming passengers, my thoughts flashed back to my military flying—life-threatening situations. None of it meant anything now. Just finding the owner of this dog, whose life seemed to be hanging on a thread, was all that stood between me and unemployment.

As I entered the baggage claim area, there she was. Although I was dripping wet with sweat, I wanted to appear calm and in control of the situation, so I stopped running. I walked the last few yards through the crowd to where she stood.

She seemed to pay me no notice as I placed the cage next to her. However, with a quick glance she noticed her dog, now with both eyes open, attempting to sit up. I was trying to conceal my overwhelming joy that somehow I had saved this dog's life, when the passenger looked at me with much disappointment and said, "He's awake, I guess I didn't sedate him enough."

Michael Thorstenson
Captain
Miami

Gotcha!

Bob Hope stepped up to my ticket counter at the San Diego Airport—he was purchasing his own ticket and checking in his own luggage. He was also joking with me about our airline, so I decided to joke back.

With a straight face, I told him that his flight would be a little longer than usual because, in cooperation with the Air Force, we would be towing a target behind our plane for them to shoot at, and the extra weight would slow us down.

With that explanation, he left my counter and walked around the corner to the gate. A few seconds later, after he had fully processed what I had just said, he came back around the corner with a big grin on his face and said, "You got me!" I could hear him laughing all the way down the ramp—a real gentleman and nice guy.

Edward Novak
Retired Ticket Agent
San Diego

A Child's Wisdom

I once took my daughters, ages 16, 14 and 10, on an American Airlines trip. For the two youngest, it was their first flight.

There was some turbulence on part of the journey, and at one point the pilot dipped the plane to the left and then to the right. When my 14-year-old asked what he was doing, my 10-year-old put her hands on her hips and answered loudly and somewhat indignantly, "He's changing lanes, silly!"

This response prompted some long and almost loud laughter from many of the buttoned-down businessmen sitting near us.

Somehow, word of my daughter's "explanation" reached the cockpit. After we landed and were exiting the plane, the pilots told my daughter Laura how she had made a bumpy flight memorable and funny. For Laura, this was a big moment. She felt so smart, and she hasn't forgotten how the flight crew made her feel special.

Cathleen Griffin
Domestic AAdvantage Agent
Dallas/Fort Worth

You Just Can't Make This Stuff Up

Just when you think you've heard it all, life gives you another surprise!

Ground Services received a call from a captain who had just landed in Las Vegas. A woman had accidentally dropped her false teeth down the toilet. We were requested to back pump the holding tank and try to find her teeth. (I hope no one in Passenger Service ever tells me they do more for our customer than we do!) We found the teeth, cleaned them up and the woman couldn't have been happier. Only one problem: they had turned blue!

Vincent McGonagle
Ramp Service
Las Vegas

A Special Serenade

Sometimes, there are benefits to bad weather.

I remember a particularly cold and stormy night at the Buffalo airport. All flights were grounded, with nothing coming in or going out. We had already loaded passengers for a flight to La Guardia, and were told that the weather was supposed to improve. The passengers were told to remain onboard. This usually doesn't help morale, and the passengers were a bit uneasy.

But there was a special bonus that night. Perry Como, the famous singer, was onboard, and he volunteered to sing a medley to pass the time.

You can imagine how appreciative the "captive audience" was and how quickly the time passed.

The weather broke, and everyone got to New York a little late, but happy, with a lifetime memory of a special concert. What a wonderful treat for us all!

Edward Novak
Retired Ticket Agent
San Diego

An Evening with God

Once, when I was flying into Nashville, we had George Burns on our plane. He had completed filming his second *Oh God* movie and he asked me to join him for dinner. As he was traveling with his business manager, he asked if I would invite one of our other flight attendants to join us. We went to a lovely restaurant and had a wonderful evening.

When we returned home, I told the story to my minister's wife. She called into the other room to tell her husband, "Teddy had dinner with God!"

Teddy Ann Tallon
International Flight Attendant
Dallas/Fort Worth

Humor Makes the Time Go Quickly

I remember a flight from Phoenix to Washington-Dulles, loaded with a bunch of doctors returning from a convention. They were in a real party-time mood—there was a lot of laughter and joking going on in the Main Cabin.

I had just finished passing out hot towels and was heading back up to the front of the cabin to begin collecting them when I heard snickering behind me. When I turned around, the doctors were holding up their hands as if they had just scrubbed and were ready for surgery! That prank had the whole plane in good spirits for the rest of the flight and reminded me how good humor can really make time pass so quickly.

There is a post script. After we landed at Dulles, I was driving back to my apartment when I got a flat tire. I had gotten out of my car and was trying to figure out how to change the tire when a car pulled up. Guess who? One of my doctor passengers had stopped to help me. He changed my tire for me and went on his way.

It's memories like this that make life with American Airlines worthwhile and fulfilling.

Cynthia Drey
Flight Attendant
Chicago-O'Hare

"Prop Wash"

I started with American as a secretary in the Safety division. Its offices were located above the hangar. One day, as a practical joke, my supervisor asked me to go down to the hangar to get a bucket of "prop wash." At the time, I imagined dragging a bucket of soapy water back to the office. Little did I know that "prop wash" is a technical term that means the "wind" from a spinning propeller. Needless to say our facilities maintenance crew roared when I approached our mechanics with my enthusiastic request. Never was I happier to be the butt of a practical joke. I was accepted into the American "family" and my morale has been great ever since.

Celeste Harrington
Retired Secretary, Passenger Service
New York-Kennedy

My Reluctant Passenger

Just about any airline employee can tell you about "reluctant" passengers. We've all had our share. The key is to find what it will take to make them happy.

Several years ago at Newark, the ramp crew was loading cargo on a flight to Los Angeles. Somehow, a large German Shepherd escaped from his cage. After a hectic chase, we finally collared the dog and attempted to coax him back into his confinement. Not a chance! The dog was terrified of his surroundings and totally refused to cooperate. We tried every trick we knew, but couldn't return the dog to the cage. With departure time only moments away, we became desperate.

Then, with inspiration I wish I had all the time, I ran upstairs to the cabin and asked our First Class flight attendant for a steak. Puzzled, but sensing my desperation, she surrendered the meat, and I dashed back down to the tarmac. I held the steak in front of the dog's nose and he followed me right into the cage to wolf down his First Class meal.

Fred Garmont
Retired Supervisor, Ramp Service
Newark

Commuter Life Isn't Boring

I received the following letter from one of our first officers at JFK. Let me just add this disclaimer: we are not making fun of our passengers or making light of an embarrassing situation, but I think it is important to know that sometimes it's okay to smile at life's unique encounters:

Two of my fellow pilots and I were the last to deplane the American Eagle flight, and seemed to have our own bus to take us to the terminal. One lone passenger was about to board the bus when gusty winds lifted his toupee vertically and sent it rolling down the Eagle ramp. Before he could react, his hairpiece was 20 feet away. The man gave chase, but the toupee was very "hair-o-dynamic," rolling across the ramp like a Frisbee, with ever-increasing speed. The three of us stood watching as this poor man ran on to the main taxiway chasing his hair.

Concerned for his safety and wanting to help, we grabbed the man's carry-ons, boarded the bus, and instructed the bus driver to, "follow that hair!" After several hundred yards, we passed the man, but his wig was still in front of us. I told the driver that since the ramp was clear, and the toupee was obviously important to the man, that I would jump off the bus and help him.

As I hopped out of the bus, the elusive wig was several feet from me, closing at a rate faster than I could react to. The next thing I knew, I had replaced the hapless passenger, giving chase to an elusive toupee determined to tour the entirety of JFK. I finally stopped the perpetrator, but as I bent down to pick it up, I lifted my foot and the receding hairline bolted 20 feet downwind, and I was on the chase again. Through wind and driving rain, I could hear my fellow aviators laughing hysterically from the pursuing bus.

As the wig continued, I saw that it would soon blow over the bridge and across runway 13R. I was feeling desperate. Finally, the break I needed arrived as a large, deep, water puddle slowed the flying bonnet. I lunged one last desperate time, my foot pinning the culprit in several inches of water.

With soggy trophy in hand, I waited for the bus to pick me up. Our distressed passenger, obviously humiliated, mumbled his gratitude. He said he would have let it go, but it cost $300. He lamented that he should have used better glue, and something about "life's most embarrassing moment."

Who said a commuter life was boring?

Captain Cecil D. Ewell, Jr.
Chief Pilot
Vice President, Flight

For Every Problem There Is a Solution

Severe lightning erupted at the Milwaukee Airport shortly before a flight to Chicago was due to leave. Heavy rains and strong winds caused a power outage in the terminal. Determined to have their Chicago passengers depart on time, agents used flashlights to escort passengers down the now-darkened jetbridge for boarding. Then the real problem was discovered.

The weight of over 100 passengers had caused the airplane to lower by almost a foot (a normal occurrence). However, without electric power, agents could not regulate the height of the jetbridge, nor back it away from the plane. The door of the plane could not be closed without bumping into the floor of the jetbridge. Authorities estimated at least an hour before the airport could expect a return of power to enable them to re-position the jetbridge.

This was unacceptable to one quick-thinking flight attendant. She had an idea, and after receiving approval from the captain, she executed her plan.

In a PA announcement to all passengers, she identified the problem in detail. She continued, "So, this is one of those adventures you'll tell your friends and family about for years to come. Would everyone please stand and move as far to the rear of the plane as possible? If we can shift enough weight to the back of the plane, the front might just lift up enough for our agent to clear the jetbridge and close the door."

Over 100 passengers moved to the rear and the nose lifted more than enough for the agent to close the door.

The aircraft carefully backed away from the bridge and the flight arrived in Chicago on time with over 100 satisfied passengers with fond memories of a very clever flight attendant.

Editor

A Macho Moment

In an effort to expedite a rapid change of crews for another departure, I offered to retrieve some personal items that one of our flight attendants had left onboard our previous aircraft.

Much to my surprise, it was a partially completed knit sweater along with a big ball of yarn and knitting needles.

As a captain in uniform, I, obviously, took the correct action: I hid the entire thing under my uniform raincoat and, holding it in place with my left arm, walked directly into the Christmas rush at Kennedy Airport.

As I was proceeding to our gate, suddenly the ball of yarn rolled from under my raincoat down the ramp and got tangled in several passengers' feet. As they tugged and tripped the yarn only rolled further!

Roosevelt Greer, the former NFL football star, stopped and picked up "my" yarn. He followed the string to "my" knitting, and as he handed me back the ball of yarn, he commented, "Interesting hobby you have there, Captain."

The good news is we departed on time.

Donald R. Mayo
Retired Captain
Boston Airport

I've Got Your Number

One day I received a call from an older gentleman who asked me if this was the number for "Air Quality Control of Los Angeles." I told him he had reached the American Airlines reservations line. I could hear the frustration in his voice. This, apparently, was his second attempt to reach the Air Quality Control office, and he kept getting American Airlines instead. I mentioned that maybe "someone upstairs" was trying to tell him something. I explained to him that we had just announced a special fare from Los Angeles to Honolulu, and that he might want to consider—or he might need (I joked)—a vacation. His voice began to soften when he said, "You know, that's where my wife and I went on our honeymoon 35 years ago, and we are having an anniversary soon. What a surprise that would be for her!" With a quick, romantic impulse, he decided to book the trip to Honolulu. I gladly took the reservation and ticketed the pair!

As we were saying our good-byes, I did thank him for calling American. He hesitated and asked, rather meekly, "You wouldn't happen to have the telephone number of Air Quality Control for Los Angeles?" It wasn't as easy as booking a flight, but I got it for him.

Evelyn M. Hicks
International AAdvantage Reservations Agent
Southern Reservations Office
Dallas/Fort Worth

Be Professional

My hat goes off to all the American Airlines crew members I have worked with who have shown such amazing talent for working with sometimes difficult passengers.

We were ready to leave Boston for Chicago when a passenger rushed onboard, stowed his bag, and literally snapped his fingers at a flight attendant.

"Hey, waitress, gimme a scotch and soda!"

Without missing a beat, the flight attendant said, "I'm sorry, sir, but you've missed your flight."

Confused, the passenger asked, "Isn't this the flight to Chicago?"

"Why, yes, it is" she answered. "But the 'Gimme Flight' left an hour ago. This is the 'Please,' 'May I' and 'Thank You' flight."

"Oh," he replied sheepishly. "May I have a scotch and soda, please?"

Airline travel is serious business and this young lady brought a really professional atmosphere into the cabin. I have always marveled at how our well-trained crews could turn an upset, angry and sometimes rude passenger into a smiling, pleasant and loyal friend of American Airlines.

Tony Felder
Retired Captain
Miami

All in a Day's Work

I work in Toronto Cargo. Once, after our last flight had arrived from La Guardia, I was paged by our baggage service agent searching for two brown cartons that might have been inadvertently mixed with cargo. The two cartons contained Sesame Street Muppets that belonged to Jim Henson. Mr. Henson was waiting in the baggage office.

Sure enough, we had the cartons. I called our baggage agent and told her that the cartons were on their way. About 20 minutes later, I was paged again by our baggage agent still looking for the cartons. I told her one of our people had taken them back a while ago. I then paged our cargo runner who confirmed he had immediately put the cartons on the baggage belt. I asked the runner to meet me outside the Customs hall so that we could find the now missing cartons.

When I asked him to show me "exactly" where he put the cartons, he pointed to the belt marked "U.S. Customs." This was the wrong belt. We were not sure where this belt even ended-up! I decided that the quickest thing to do was to simply get on the belt and see if it would take us to the cartons. The runner looked at me in total disbelief. The belt went up a 45 degree incline into the rafters of the terminal and neither of us knew where we would land.

So there we were, two grown men riding the belt and ducking the girders on the ceiling, heading toward who knows where. I had visions of coming to the end and sliding down into some carousel in front of hundreds of passengers and being led away by Customs for questioning!

Finally, we arrived at our destination—the U.S. Customs counter. Thank God it was late, and no Customs agents were nearby. Lo and behold, the missing cartons were there on the floor, beside the belt.

We picked up the cartons and returned them to our baggage service office, but our agents were nowhere to be found. Rather than leaving them unattended again, we decided to take them back to Cargo, where we would call our agents to let them know that we had the cartons.

When we called the baggage agent to say we had finally retrieved the cartons, she was skeptical as to whether we really had them. After I told her of our adventure through the airport, she began to laugh hysterically.

She then explained that while we were riding the belt, the baggage agents had gone searching for the cartons, and had found them on the Customs belt. Because Mr. Henson had already gone to his hotel, they decided to leave them next to the baggage belt (where the runner and I found them) so that they could go and get coffee. When they returned, to their alarm, the bags had once again disappeared, because the runner and I had carried them back to Cargo!

Everything ended up all right, and we all had a good laugh about our incredible quest for the missing Muppets. I guess it's all in a day's work!

Tony Volpe
Lead Agent, Cargo
Toronto

Peanuts

Pulitzer prize-winning columnist George F. Will once wrote an article that appeared in the *Tulsa Daily World* opposing airline deregulation, a view supported by most carriers in 1977.

However, Will began the article with a scolding for American Airlines because he could not obtain a second bag of peanuts on an AA flight. Because of this, Will stated he would begin flying a competitor who featured macadamia nuts.

AA employee Chris Bearden, Engineering, Tulsa, took exception to this and wrote Mr. Will the following letter:

Dear Mr. Will,

We enjoyed your article, "Deregulating Airlines," which was published by the *Tulsa Daily World* here in Oklahoma. In the article you stated that you are now a United Airlines customer because American Airlines refused you a second packet of peanuts on our flight.

We want you back flying our airline. Therefore, several employees have taken a collection to buy you the enclosed peanuts. Fly again with American and bring these with you. We are proud of our on-time performance and safety record. We don't want to lose a good customer for a bag of peanuts.

Sincerely,
Chris Bearden
AA Employee

Some weeks later, Will wrote back from his Washington office:

> Dear Mr. Bearden
>
> Thanks. All is forgiven. I am on my way to San Diego on American Airlines.
>
> Sincerely,
> George F. Will

Voluntary Separation

One very busy Sunday, the agent working next to me checked in a passenger who arrived minutes after cut-off time for baggage. While we do all we can to accommodate a late passenger, bags pose a bit of a challenge and sometimes have to be checked on the next flight. When the agent advised the passenger that we wouldn't have time to load his luggage and that it had to be checked with a "voluntary separation" tag, he responded, "Is that like a divorce?" I explained it was "a lot less expensive" and we all had a good laugh.

J.A. Caudle
Ticket Agent
Miami

Sorry, Right Number

As an AAdvantage reservations agent, I often deal with passengers who are almost as knowledgeable about air travel as I am.

But occasionally, I'll get a call from a customer wanting to change a reservation or check on a flight on another airline.

Invariably, I'll get the embarrassed response, "Oh no! I called the wrong airline."

My response? "No, you didn't. You called the RIGHT airline, you just booked your reservation on the WRONG one!"

They usually respond laughing, "You got that right!"

Never underestimate the power of humor. Laughter is so good for us—healthy for our physical, spiritual and emotional selves, as well as for our greater corporate "body"!

JoAnn Jurries
AAdvantage Reservations Agent
Tucson

You're Ours!

Despite some disagreements through the years, members of American's trade unions truly are proud to be a part of the American family. They may get somewhat vocal about management from time to time, but they do their job better than anyone in the business.

American's pilots are the backbone of the airline and contribute greatly to the quality and success of our airline. One time, during a heated question and answer session with Mr. Crandall, a group of pilots besieged him with hardball financial questions. Crandall, an efficient numbers man, parried all their questions convincingly in an intelligent and friendly manner.

At the end of the difficult meeting one newly converted, and now supportive, captain stood up and said, "Mr. Crandall, you know we all think you're a son of a bitch, but we're sure glad you're *our* son of a bitch and not a competitor's."

Art Jackson
Retired Director
Corporate Communications
Headquarters

You See Some Amazing Things at the Airport

One of my most unique experiences at American came when I was working a Las Vegas departure.

A passenger approached me with a trained orangutan that acted like it was a human! The man spoke to the ape and it seemed to understand everything he said.

The passenger then asked me to hold the orangutan's hand while he went to make a phone call. The orangutan, upset with his owner's departure, crossed its arms, sat down, pouted its lips and seemed very unhappy. From my experience training animals I decided that I had better take control of the situation. Engaging the ape in "conversation," I asked her if she liked airplanes. She shook her head "No!" and put her arm around my neck—we were friends.

When the man returned he was very pleased with my handling of the orangutan. Saying our goodbyes, the ape leaned over for a kiss. I extended my hand and told her, "A handshake will do." The ape was not amused.

I accepted her affections and from then on, the passenger specifically requested me to handle his orangutan whenever they came through.

Now that's really customer satisfaction!

Richard Cunningham
Fleet Service Clerk
Dallas/Fort Worth

Haste Makes Waste

I remember a situation when I was the manager of aircraft maintenance at Boston. Al Casey was president of AA at the time and he visited our station frequently.

Whenever someone as important as the president of your company visits, it is essential that everything go well. On this particular visit, everything went very well. Well, almost.

Typically, Casey would conduct business right up to departure time and board the aircraft within the last few minutes of scheduled departure.

He was more than typically late this day and was being escorted briskly to the departure gate by one of our passenger service supervisors. They reached the gateway just as the door was about to close. Those who were seeing him off wished him well and breathed a sigh of relief.

Casey was en route to Washington, D.C. and we all knew that was usually very important business. It wasn't until about one hour later when we realized that, in our haste, we had put him on a flight to Chicago.

William Culhane
Vice President, Line Maintenance
Tulsa

ACKNOWLEDGMENTS

As a former American employee, I have enjoyed the experience of creating this book tremendously. It has brought back many good memories, re-introduced me to lots of old friends, and helped me to better appreciate the more important things employees in every company should focus on in their day to day employment . . . regardless of which company they work for, what they do, whether their name is on the outside of their office door or their shirt pocket.

In an earlier book, I mentioned that if you really enjoy your work, you add five extra days to your weekend. This attitude is shared by so many of the people I have met at American Airlines—and it comes through very strongly in the letters you will read in this book.

I wish to acknowledge and thank the thousands of American employees who thought enough about their company to write. I strongly regret that we did not have enough space to accommodate every letter sent to us.

I would also like to thank Bob Crandall and Don Carty for their courage in moving forward with this book. Obviously they had no idea what employees would send in . . . but they both had confidence that American employees share an exceptional pride in their company, and that we would receive some outstanding submissions. They were both right.

My thanks to Anne McNamara, general counsel at American, for guiding me through the legal process of "dotting the i's and crossing the t's" for this book with a level of professionalism I have never seen in my 30 years of being in business. This is truly an amazing woman! My comment to her was: "You sure don't act like a lawyer." Her comment to me was: "Thank you!"

A special thanks goes to Mike Gunn, senior vice president marketing, who has been a colleague and personal friend for almost three decades. Mike has done so much for American. His loyalty to the employees and the company is unparalleled. It was a pleasure working with him, and, I am quite sure, we would not have as fine a book as we have without his valuable input.

Thank you to Paul Gold, and his assistant Billy Hall, who spent hours researching valuable materials for the book.

This book is about "great people at American" with "great attitudes." The "Acknowledgements" chapter is as good a place as any to mention my thanks to Karaleen Eichorst, assistant to Mr. Crandall. I had flown to Dallas to visit the C.R. Smith Museum as a part of my research, and found that without a car, it is almost impossible to get to the museum from American's headquarters.

The company van does not go there, and the fare is too small for a taxi to want to take you. Karaleen did not hesitate a moment and said, "Let's go, I'll take you." I felt a little guilty bumming a ride from the chairman's assistant . . . but then, she works for American Airlines, and this book is all about people like her.

It gets better. When I finished my work at the C.R. Smith Museum (which, I might add, is an amazing place to visit if you are ever in the Dallas area), I had the "ride" problem in reverse. How was I now going to get back to the headquarters building? The young lady at the desk recommended I take the company limo to the airport and then catch the company limo from the airport to the headquarters building. I estimated this process would take about 1-1/2 hours with the transfers and all. She also said, "Don't call a taxi. They won't come out. The fare is too small." "I've heard this." I replied.

I could see the headquarters building from the museum. It was about a mile away—separated from the museum by a big cow pasture. As I was contemplating walking across the cow pasture a complete stranger came along and said, "You look like you need a ride . . . where are you going?" "Over to the headquarters building" I told him.

"Well I'm not going that way, but it's only a mile or two out of my way. Come on, I'll take you."

My new driver, Presley Donaldson, an international flight instructor, certainly did not know who I was. He is just the kind of person that would stop to help you change a tire in the middle of the night. He is also a typical example of the people you will read about in this book.

Thank you, Presley, for being such a nice person and for taking the time to go out of your way to help me. I would fly on your airplane anytime.

Some of my biggest thanks go to our staff; Annmarie Godwin, my assistant and right hand; Laura Cuddy, our managing director; Barry Hoffman, our executive editor along with Kim Pendarvis and Carrie Wittenstein, our editors, who all did so much to coordinate almost 4,000 letters from dedicated American employees into this book.